The Emancipation of a Buried Man

A MEMOIR BY EDDY GILMORE

D1501627

Delivered by bike
by
Eddy Gilmore

This is a work of nonfiction. In some instances, names, locations, and other identifying details have been changed to protect individual privacy.

Cover art by Shawna Gilmore
Designed by Naomi Christenson

TABLE OF CONTENTS

PART ONE: LOST

LOST AMONG THE PILES

We did not intend to hoard the feces, but once a home gets beyond a certain point in terms of filth, you cease to be repulsed. It was simply our reality.

Our situation had become so bad that Mom and I cleaned the house in a near panic the day the assessor came to inspect the house for tax valuation purposes. We feared the horrid conditions could be reported to child protective services, with me ultimately being removed from the home. Right up to the moment the gentleman knocked at the door, with no time to resolve the full extent of the problem, I was sweeping a significant supply of dried dog poop behind an open door. It had piled up in our hot and sunny laundry room, dried to a crisp, for months on end. The doggy doo was Death-Valley-dry and had turned white, which is the calcium left over after all the water evaporates. It crunched into hundreds of shards of smithereens when stepped on.

The chaotic and confusing state of my house mirrored my childhood. The word messy doesn't begin to describe the situation. My mother and I lived in a small house on a concrete slab without a basement or attic, but we had more junk packed into that place than the total accumulation of ten average homes. No doors could open all the way, and on some occasions one was reduced to sliding through a doorway sideways in order to fit through a 10 - 12 inch gap. It was abject squalor, filth, and a sub-human existence brought on by obsessive hoarding of the most extreme variety that I have come across.

Piles reaching to the ceiling behaved like landfills as long forgotten items molded and rotted away deep within. The effluent produced from decomposing and festering food, dog excrement and urine, layered within these archaeological-like dumping grounds kept the carpet continually moist. If I made the mistake of walking in bare feet my soles turned as black as night.

To this day, I have difficulty walking in any home without slippers. I routinely carry them with me in my jacket pockets while walking a mile through snow and ice to watch Packers' games with a friend. I believe I will bring them along if I'm ever invited to visit with the First Family at the White House. An unexpected step into a small spill of water immediately reminds me of squishing onto a carpet drenched in dog pee. Since our carpets were laid directly onto the concrete slab without a pad of any sort, it became especially gross like a puddle in places. Years of this rendered our carpet a biohazard.

The landscape of each room varied, but each was marked by similar undulations between the towering peaks, which occasionally collapsed as an avalanche of detritus on me or Mom. Typically we'd be sitting in the one or two open spots eating dinner in front of the television when gravity came calling.

Throughout my early childhood the house was messy, but livable. However, Mom seems to have coped with the stress of caring for me with minuscule resources by nurturing a hoarding habit that eventually overwhelmed her. Her hoarding has behaved like Seymour, the flesh-eating plant from the cult classic movie *Little Shop of Horrors*. I imagine that it seemed like a harmless idiosyncrasy at first. After all, she could not afford to be wasteful of anything. The habit eventually took on a life of its own, consuming everything around it, including me.

There were only a few unavoidable instances when unsuspecting members of the human race unknowingly crossed the threshold into bizarro world. On one occasion I was humiliated when my paper route manager came in to change his pants after a coffee spill. His expression said it all, as he had to change three feet from the opening of the front door. The shame and self-loathing felt in such a circumstance is difficult to describe, and impossible to quantify. These were unthinkable instances to avoid at all costs. By way of comparison, I was far less embarrassed—though the experience came complete with pointing and laughing—when my babysitter's daughters got a clear, unobstructed view of my ding-a-ling one afternoon. The importance of wearing underwear underneath shorts hadn't been communicated to me. This also was a problem in school with a pair of overalls once, but we need not go down that path yet.

My babysitter was a raging bitch. There is no other word for it. I have never met another individual in my entire life who was as persistently mean to kids. She was horribly cruel to her stepdaughters, whom she belittled and insulted to the point of Cinderella-like abuse. Two of them were referred to as *ugly* on a daily basis. She brought the eldest girl in middle school to tears on multiple occasions by publicly calling her *flat-chested*. I witnessed this at least 50 times.

On one occasion it was necessary for me to dine with the entire family at the table. The experience was miserable, as it ushered me further into the torture chamber of abuse that these poor girls were forced to endure. Sitting at the table was horrible. Normally we were kept outside to fend for ourselves. Being confined to the kitchen, unable to escape, was frightening. You were exposed to obsessive, ever-watchful, vigilant eyes that were demonic in intensity. The atmosphere caused you to huddle into your shell while keeping your eyes on your food to escape notice. Speaking, and thus drawing attention to yourself, was as unthinkable and potentially fatal as if doing so in a North Korean prison camp. On this particular evening one of the girls apparently succumbed to a lapse in judgment by politely remarking in a mouse-like voice that the butter on her potatoes was moldy.

The stepmother flew into a rage reminiscent of the Queen of Hearts from Alice in Wonderland, who would have decreed judgment saying, "Off with her head!" Her screaming and devilish looking eyes fixated on the poor girl still stand out in my memory, as does the child's unending weeping afterwards. Suffice it to say, the defenseless adolescent ate her potato. She was forced to scrape up every last bit of mold, grease, skin, globs of fat from the rest of the meal, and shove it down her gullet. That plate was wiped clean, and she can count herself lucky for not having her mouth washed out with soap. Palmolive dish soap was the usual soap du jour for any backtalk, and it would have been swallowed afterward. I am quite certain this was a normal course of events at the dinner table. The real crime of it all was that the disengaged father failed to intervene in the least. The child was thoroughly broken, and came undone with sobs that would not cease. After the "Queen's" hollering to shut up failed to deliver the desired effect, she ordered her to "Get out of my face!"

For some reason she generally left the pretty one alone, aside from the occasional snide remark like, "She thinks her shit don't stink." This wicked stepmother ruled the house with an iron fist. Her husband was largely withdrawn, an apparent alcoholic, and was typically away at work, sleeping, fishing, or drinking. He seemed to be most engaged when disciplining his three daughters from another marriage, which always came in the form of a fit of rage with his leather belt. The girls would tell me how many times they were hit with it, which was frankly a whip, and sometimes the belt buckle delivered the entry point of the blow.

When this woman, my alleged "care-giver" while my mom was at work, stopped over to speak with my mom on one occasion, she blamed me for the condition of the house. Though Mom was standing next to me, she peered quizzically into my eyes—a little kid in third or fourth grade—and said, "Why don't you clean this shit up?"

I must say, however, that there was great good that came out of being mired within the "care" of this family for five long years. It helped me see that things could always be worse. It doesn't seem possible, but the babysitter's extended family actually was worse. It was riddled with ignorance, alcoholism, endless profanity, screaming, and abuse. Amidst 110-decibel-level screaming strewn with obscenities (like abandoned tires along a polluted, muddy river), the large hulk of a stepdad repeatedly slammed a difficult third grade boy into a wall with such force that the child's body broke the wall between the studs. His full body left an indentation in the interior wall, as he violently cried from the overwhelming stress and pain.

This family originally lived a half-hour north of us in Milwaukee, and I vividly remember the long trip to visit them. The drive was an unending purgatory-like experience. All the kids were crammed into the back seat of the hot car, and I secretly enjoyed sitting on the lap of one of the older girls during the journey. Three adults chain-smoked in the front seat with the windows closed. I sat on a bony lap while struggling to breathe with my t-shirt and hands cupped over my mouth and nose in order to somehow avoid the dense eye-burning cigarette smoke. This enraged my babysitter. She demanded that I breathe normally. It was unwise to sass back or question a direct order from her.

Arriving in the scary inner city of Milwaukee continued to add to the general anxiety. The day dragged on forever amidst the yelling, drinking, and scant shade of a tiny backyard that was dominated by a cracked and weedy concrete patio. I tried to put myself in a happier place by studying any insects I could find while turning over every conceivable stone or scrap of wood. I left them untouched and imagined the world from their view. At the time I was grateful this family lived so far away, but the next year they moved into my little neighborhood of Caddy Vista out in the country. I swear the property values of the neighboring homes must have dropped in half, as did any serenity the poor occupants once enjoyed.

Though my parents had their problems, I never wanted to trade them in for the alternatives I was exposed to. This was a worthwhile lesson that continues to benefit me today.

DISCLAIMER

Mom will read this recollection of my childhood. The prospect frightens me because I genuinely love and care for her. The intent here is not to engage in a slash-and-burn style rant. I am merely telling my story as it happened. I have come to the conclusion that the burden should not be on me to remain silent. I have learned a great deal from my past experiences, and continue to do so in fact. They are foundational to what I need to convey here. My mother is no different from other parents, in that she wants the best for me. As a child I never doubted her love. I knew from an early age that she experienced significant problems in her past that she has never been able to overcome. Life has never been easy for her. I don't blame her, or Dad for that matter, for my difficult childhood. It is simply my story. I have learned to accept it for what it is, and glean important pearls of wisdom that I believe most people take for granted.

8

2

SMELLS

Recently I received a box in the mail from Mom containing my old children's picture bible. My dad gave it to me when I was about the same age my kids are now. The smell of the pages defies belief. The space between the covers smells exactly like the old house that I oh-so-rarely visit now. Acting as a sponge, the accumulated stench of 27 years was compressed between its covers, stirring memories that I prefer lie dormant. That, and the immediate impact of mold on our family's allergies when the pages were opened, forced me to relegate it to the garbage bin outside. In a small passing way, the effect resembled that of the lost Ark of the Covenant being opened in the climactic scene from the Indiana Jones movie, *Raiders of the Lost Ark*.

For this reason I have very few childhood mementos to share with my son and daughter, who are twins, and who are wildly interested in stories from my past. Unfortunately these stories are rarely unearthed. Perhaps I've bottled them up, or they may have been bound up with all the dirty secrets of the past and cast into an abyss with a millstone to hold them down.

The rank smell of decomposition filled our house. It accumulated and was stored up like an angry genie in a bottle. Immediately upon opening the front door, even while you were still outside in the fresh air, the potent putrescence hit you like a freight train while overloading your senses. The fetid reek was the unholy offspring produced from a veritable kingdom of mold combined with years of dust layered like sediment throughout the house where there were virtually no flat surfaces from which to remove it. Dog excrement, urine, and vomit, hidden in corners and crannies in various states of decomposition, further complemented this one-of-a-kind diabolical mixture. Rounding out the reek were the rot and decay of every conceivable organic material. Due to these conditions I repeatedly developed extreme bouts of bronchitis, and asthma.

I literally cannot remember a single pleasant smell in the house. Such aromas commonly lingered in the homes of my friends, and I delighted in them as a flower lover might pause and bend low in an arboretum to take a deep breath of an especially gorgeous, rare, and elusive bloom. My friends always took these smells for granted, but I never did. Fresh apple pies or cookies pulled from the oven, homemade pizza, or even a whiff of the pleasant essence of cleanliness, were never lost on me. I continue to be blessed with a marvelous ability to appreciate such small things to this day.

More importantly, however, the general atmosphere within my home and life prevented any flowering of my character. The effect on me was a persistent stifling that went on for years.

3

ON THE SUBJECT OF FOOD

We ate incredibly poorly. There were no healthy meals in my house. I microwaved copious amounts of pizza pockets. Fresh produce was scarce. Anything perishable tended to rot in the refrigerator or under the mounds of boxes and other garbage that covered every square inch of the kitchen table to an average depth of one to two feet. The countertop was likewise burdened with detritus, as was perhaps 80% of the floor.

Enough food to feed an army has been lost in limbo over the years. A thin covering of debris would render it forever forgotten. Sometimes the hungry sea of chaos seemed to swallow the food whole. This made for a miserable situation in the summertime especially. The home was impossibly hot and stuffy. Food lost in limbo, such as a misplaced hamburger, raw bacon, or cantaloupe, did not last long. When any non-processed food rotted, it didn't simply turn brown or green. The decay advanced like an army on an unsuspecting populace. Putrefaction was so complete that any shape or form resembling its previous life had long since been extinguished. The collection of rapidly obliterating molecules looked like something from deep within a compost pile. Sometimes the gelatinous goo or dark fluids had thoroughly run their course, leaving only a monument to the work of bacteria in the form of a thick stain. If the food fell into the blob a caramel-like compound permanently worked into the fibers of denim jeans, into multiple skeins of yarn, and dripped between the covers of books and magazines. Gravity, that old bastard, added a flourishing touch by causing it to ooze down one of the unseen sides of the couch.

Tidying up the kitchen involved removing paper bags containing unpacked groceries that had fused to the floor. The entire contents and bottom of the bag rotted into the divots and cracks that separated the tiles. When lifting the bag, only the sides pulled up to expose a serious mess. It sounds crazy, but cleaning the kitchen was preferable to all the other rooms, because it involved the least amount of decision-making.

Other rooms were filled with Mom's clothes, unopened craft supplies, books that went unread, numerous tissue boxes, toilet paper, family keepsakes like photo albums and scrapbooks, endless oddities, important documents like my birth certificate or Mom's social security card, occasional valuables, bras, socks, even money. I could never figure out where to put everything.

The kitchen was simple. Everything needing to be tossed was extremely obvious. Produce rotted. Milk curdled. There were fascinating packages of foodstuffs to study that had gone uneaten for a decade or longer. Even sealed bags of flour and cereals crawled with bugs. I could really make a difference in there by hauling out three or four large garbage bags in short order. Clearing space to open the refrigerator door more completely was particularly satisfying, but this then required cleaning out the fridge as well. I'd clear myself a generous notch between the debris to eat cereal at the kitchen table. This was tantamount to pulling the king's throne out of storage, because then I didn't have to sit on the couch and spill all over myself prior to catching the bus for school. It was nearly impossible to give the counters and stovetop a full Betty Crocker clean. The encrusted barnacles were too entrenched to wipe or scrub away. This was particularly a problem with the 1950's era stove that was original to the house. At some point the oven quit working. Mom kept it for years afterwards.

For a real adventure I delved into the adjoining room that had been added as an addition to the house. This room went unheated and was generally closed off. Therefore the temperatures ranged from stifling hot to very cold. Mom kept hundreds of canned goods back there that she obtained over the years. These were either store-bought vegetables stockpiled when they were on sale or homemade applesauce in quart-sized Mason jars. Often the rusty metal cans bulged or were severely dented. These were likely cesspools of botulism, and there were always severely discolored jars of applesauce to cull. An extra freezer was housed in the far rear corner that was sometimes impossible to reach. The innards were encased in a huge blob of frost that swallowed up the contents like ancient mastodons. I wonder what it cost my mom to run that energy hog in the high heat of summer.

Getting back there to find old slimy popsicles was a trick. The back door from the kitchen was usually blocked, and then once opened the smell from the sealed up back room made the rest of the house, which may have had an open window at least, smell relatively refreshing in comparison. The room was stuffed to capacity, so getting back to the freezer involved shimmying sideways between abandoned pieces of furniture and canned goods, while also being careful to watch your step for dog poop since the dog would sneak back there if the door was left open.

The malnutrition and over-abundance of sub-par processed food caused me to have an undying love affair with well-prepared and presented fresh vegetables and meat. Whenever I visited my grandparents I luxuriated in the inexhaustible supply of healthy food. I never took for granted Grandmother's hard work preparing large serving bowls of potatoes, broccoli, peas, and a scrumptious roast or stew. On the contrary, I am certain I partook in those meals with more gratitude and joy than anyone else fortunate enough to have sat at that table over the seven decades she had labored in the kitchen on the corner of Jackson and Metonga Avenue in Crandon, Wisconsin.

The majority of produce was fresh from their garden, and I spent most of each day with them in that amazing wellspring of abundance. I adored the entire experience. Those times of eating and talking around the dinner table are among my most cherished childhood memories. These visits were relatively few and far between, because they lived five hours away. Also, it was Dad's family. Mom was not on good terms with my father, and couldn't even speak to him without yelling or uttering profanity. The wounds never healed there, and are an example of how her inability to forgive and move on have been crippling. I was fortunate enough, however, to spend an entire week with them for about three summers in a row until my mom put a stop to it.

These relatively few experiences shaped my concept of the ideal dinner with family, involving healthily and lovingly prepared food mingled with relaxed table talk where nobody is distracted by busy schedules or the TV. To this day I insist on a real plate eaten at the table, with ample time to linger and enjoy the company of those gathered together. Today we call it the Slow Food Movement, but this was everyday life for my grandparents.

The contrast was stark when compared to meals eaten at home with a plate containing a microwaved pot pie or TV dinner on my lap. I sat on the couch in the only logical spot to sit, often alone, in front of the television that remained on constantly. Occasionally Mom did rustle up an odd concoction of chili that seemed to be mostly macaroni noodles, hamburger, and canned tomatoes. You haven't seen anything until you've experienced that chili pot full of water (with the bottom inch having been burned) and still soaking in the sink under three days of unwashed dishes at the height of summer! Reaching down to the bottom of the sink to open the drain produced a red slimy film on my arm clear past the elbow. The drain catch was invariably loaded with filth. The experience was akin to what the clearing of a toilet clog with one's bare hands might feel like. The entire sink had to be emptied so the horrid red film could be scrubbed and rinsed off from top to bottom with additional piles of gunk scraped from the bottom prior to adding fresh water to engage in an epic dishwashing project that would leave you completely wet with sweat and disgusting dishwater. Finally finished and exhausted an hour or two later, with clean dishes stacked to dry in an uneasy leaning Tower of Pisa, you didn't even want to look at the dishes for another three days. Thus the cycle continued....

4

ALONE WITH THE ANIMALS

I spent the vast majority of my time alone among piles of belongings that often dwarfed my diminutive size. Boredom and a lack of purpose were constant companions, along with my trusted friend and brother, Curly (a poodle/terrier mix). Over the span of a few years I sought companionship in other animals, but found I never had enough of them. Eventually I developed a hoarding problem of my own.

In my bedroom, a normal childhood room measuring approximately 8 X 12 feet, I housed 45 to 50 birds that flew freely about the room, a 55 gallon aquarium containing seven large piranhas, a smaller aquarium filled with feeder goldfish to sustain them, some boring hermit crabs, and a few dozen gerbils that came from one endlessly mating pair. At the end of seventh grade, I had received one female gerbil from a science teacher whom I revered. She was a gift that kept on giving for years after I paired her with a mate. I had this weakness of feeling as if all my animals required a mate, .

so whenever I procured new ones they were always in pairs.

All these animals were kept in my room at the same time. Even with all the craziness going on, from the age of 11 or 12, I would still ride my bike four miles each way to the local flea market, Seven Mile Fair, and return with a box containing "rescued" lovebirds, finches, or parakeets, that I released into the sanctuary of my room. Once I even brought home a dead smashed cat that I found on the road while delivering newspapers. I buried it in the yard outside my bedroom window out of compassion.

Stray dogs and cats also found a way to sniff me out and turn up at the door from time to time. Mom went crazy when I did something like feed them half an expensive ring of bologna that was all cooked up and waiting on the stovetop for supper. The friendly Great Dane that wolfed down this particular meal devoured it in a single gulp without even appearing to chew the large piece of meat. Starvation had caused his ribs to become badly exposed under a thin layer of skin. Over the course of three bitterly cold nights I secretly housed the animal in our garage. Mom shrieked in terror upon discovering the enormous, ravenous dog racing toward her when she opened the door. Despite repeated protests, I continued to house animals in there occasionally, which I feared would die without my intervention. However, Mom was most despondent about her inability to keep me from bringing more and more animals into my small room.

I just loved the flurry of activity. If the door was ever opened in a hurry the resulting whirlwind of birds, feathers, and occasional droppings, seemed to suck the oxygen out of the room. I had three very large bird cages positioned at distant locations of the room like points of an isosceles triangle. The fourth corner contained a large bird feeder designed for the outdoors that held several pounds of seed. Additionally, each cage also contained ample food supplies. My feathered friends flew to all these locations, leaving spent seed hulls and bird droppings EVERYWHERE.

A pair of love birds insisted on sleeping on the top of my curtains, so the entire back side that faced the window was covered with bird poop. It never occurred to me to wash, or even clean them off. The stuff was so omnipresent that I barely noticed. Additionally, I slept on a full-sized bed that took up most of the floor space between the cages. The majority of droppings that didn't end up in the cages, which I cleaned all too infrequently, ended up on my bed. It was a gigantic target for their marksmanship whilst on the fly. Since I frequently had the blanket and sheet turned open so my urine-stained sheets could dry and air out, many of the scratchy seed hulls fell between and among the sheets and blankets.

The contents of my room provided ample fodder for the birds to satisfy their nesting instincts. They adorned the nests I provided with bits of fluff, light debris, and lengths of thread. These were gleaned from an inexhaustible supply of raw materials that seemed to push up from the soil of their forest. Once I returned home from school to find a zebra finch fluttering wildly on my pillow. Gently grasping it in my hand, I discovered it was tethered to the pillow like a kite. A thin thread had wrapped itself around the bird's leg. Unable to unwrap it from the stick-like appendage, I snipped the thread. The finch flew back to its nest with great relief. Over a period of weeks the leg turned black. Eventually it fell off and disappeared. The bird continued to live a normal life, resting on one leg as if nothing was awry.

Finches and parakeets were constantly mating and rearing young. The situation quickly spiraled out of control. I loved seeing the baby birds, but after a while I was forced to start raiding the nests for the eggs. I would take the eggs outside and smash them just to reassure myself there wasn't a well-developed embryo inside. Occasionally the opened shell revealed a tiny bird in development with a large skull and eyes. This reduced me to putting the poor thing out of its misery. I still have difficulty picturing myself crushing the skull between my fingers. After a few of those experiences I'd leave the eggs in the nest if I didn't catch them early enough, so the problem continued to grow.

The cacophony of peeping finches, screeching and chirping parakeets, and lovebirds chattering and singing to each other, was deafening at times. Confined to the small space of my room, in which the door always had to remain closed, the cumulative sounds maintained the constant status of a dull roar. Occasionally one escaped my room, which was really just a large cage or aviary itself. This was always a time-consuming disaster. The bird, or birds, flew haphazardly in confusion throughout the house, roosting on cardboard boxes at the tops of piles, slamming into windows, etc. It was nearly impossible to try and catch or steer them back into the narrow hallway that led to my room. Also, I couldn't just leave my door open for them to fly back to safety or the others would escape too. What upending chaos! Sometimes it took hours or days to finally catch them after they wore themselves out and I could climb on all fours as I scaled Everest-like peaks of debris to reach them. Once I lost one when it was swallowed up into the blob in one of the rooms. Fortunately I found it still alive, trapped in a jar nearly dehydrated to death. I was able to nurse it back to health, and it became the only tame bird of the bunch.

The 1962 movie, *Birdman of Alcatraz*, about a misunderstood inmate sentenced to life in solitary confinement, resonated powerfully with me. It was my favorite movie, because it depicted an actual federal prisoner, Robert Stroud, who had once developed a huge collection of birds and cages in his cell. His life with birds started when he took in an orphaned baby sparrow as a pet. Ultimately his collection grew to number 300 canaries, and the experience warmed his heart from that of a cold convict to an intelligent and gentle animal lover. The large numbers of birds provided for his need to be in relationships, and the man became respected as a nationally known, bona fide ornithologist due to his published books on bird diseases and treatments. The story repeatedly brought me to tears when he was forced to give up his birds forever upon a transfer to Alcatraz. He was considered a model of self-improvement and rehabilitation in the prison system, although Stroud ultimately died in prison. Obviously I drew parallels between his life and my own.

My large family of gerbils didn't tug at my heartstrings the way the birds did. The four dozen gerbils that took up residence in a 20-gallon aquarium, 10-gallon aquarium, and at one point a dark wooden toy box, were a real problem if they escaped. Of course they found a way to chew a hole and escape from the toy box, which was housed in my dreary closet. This was a debacle of epic proportions, because they roamed and hid throughout the house. It is hardly possible to describe how difficult it was to catch them among the mess. After all, they love to hide in impossible-to-reach locations, such as behind our behemoth of a stove that was never moved.

I laid out food in various places, while patiently waiting for them to come out. I lunged for them as soon as they exposed themselves, which occasionally resulted in significant bites. Once, I harshly grasped the mother gerbil, which had been out roaming for a week or more. I was overjoyed to finally catch her, but she simply bit one thumb and turned around and bit the other as well. Both bites quickly turned bright red, as if she had just taken generous bites out of a watermelon. I dropped her, and that was the last time I saw her alive. For weeks we heard her chewing or scratching around at the bottom of piles. I dismantled the mound of debris completely, all the way to the floor, but by the time I reached the bottom she was long gone. Eventually the sounds ceased, and she was forgotten. Months later I found her while going through one of my periodic purges of junk from the house. Her body was rotted and shriveled. The head was completely gone with only two tentacles where it used to be. The image stands out in my mind.

It was a relief to finally drop the last of the gerbils off at the pet store. The experience did provide an interesting example of genetics, though. The mother gerbil was a lovely light buttercup color, while the father was darker and rat-colored. Every single one of the gerbils resembled the father exactly, as his genes were obviously incredibly dominant. I was amazed that we didn't have a single lightly colored descendant. Additionally, if you held the mother over the overfilled 20-gallon aquarium that teemed with her children, they would all become violent and attack her. If I didn't remove her within seconds they would have certainly annihilated her in short order. The father they treated as one of their own. We never once had a litter produced from incest. I found this fascinating.

My large piranhas, with their ferocious teeth always showing due to their massive underbites, dashed around in panic if startled. In contrast to their fierce appearance, they are a surprisingly skittish and nervous fish. Occasionally they even jumped right out of their aquarium during panic attacks if the lid wasn't down. Once I recall hearing a thumping sound in the room. Fearing it might be a rat, I put on boots, wore gloves and a football helmet, and cautiously entered the room with a baseball bat as my weapon. It turned out to be an enormous piranha flopping around on the floor. I returned him to the safety of his own environment, which was a long 55-gallon aquarium.

This was a very large tank at four feet long, and nearly two feet high. The weight of one of these aquariums when filled with water, gravel, and fish, is approximately 625 pounds, so this was quite the operation. I also had the smaller aquarium full of five to seven dozen goldfish at a time so as to feed them consistently. One summer I was able to entirely forgo purchasing goldfish by catching and netting bullheads in the local water-filled quarry. This was highly entertaining. One of my favorite things was to turn the light of the aquarium on at night and watch the school of approximately 150 baby bullheads undulate back and forth in a wave as if they all had studied the choreography together. Slowly, throughout the summer, the piranhas whittled the school down to nothing. I was impressed that they didn't engage in a wasteful fish-eating orgy. The supply lasted a long time.

My friend Steve and I also augmented their diet by catching adult bullhead fish with a hook and line. This provided an entire day of entertainment. Before judging me for the cruelty inflicted here, please realize that I was just a boy without many clear boundaries. Mom was at work all day. I had free reign to do what I wanted. Now an adult bullhead is equipped with two significant spines (we referred to them as horns) on either side of their head that they can use to defend themselves against predators. I struggled for a long time with a bullhead clamped in the vise, while trying to remove the horns with a pair of pliers. I don't recall if I was successful at that or if I was only able to snip them down to nubbins with a pruner. I did attempt both methods. Then I placed the ten-inch fish directly into the tank with the hungry piranhas.

The capacity of a bullhead to survive under adverse conditions is nothing short of amazing. After we essentially abused the fish to remove the spines, it was dumped into the aquarium with very little life. Within a few seconds, however, it regained consciousness and actively swam in the new surroundings. At this point the piranhas simply studied their large prey, which was many times larger than what they were familiar with. After a few minutes they pulled into tight formation behind the large dominant piranha, and he attacked the bullhead by grabbing it right in its meaty midsection and shaking it. Following this first wound the others went into a full feeding frenzy. The 55 gallons of water turned blood red. For boys around the age of 12 or 13 this was unbelievable to watch.

After the initial feeding the piranhas slowly picked apart the fish at will, and we'd leave them alone for a while. One occasion is seared into my memory as being particularly surreal and cruel. My fish had picked every morsel of meat, connective tissue, and organs, of the bullhead perfectly clean right down to its brilliantly white spine. In shock I could see that the poor fish was still alive! It was floating straight up and down like a bobber, and the head was on top of the water with its mouth opening and closing to take in air. The lungs and heart were about the only things left of the fish, as was the fully intact head that still clearly identified the species. The lungs slowly filled and deflated as the bullhead quietly respirated during the last moments of life. Steve and I were racked with guilt, but quickly did the same thing again the next day.

I was responsible for all these "pets". No matter how many I accumulated into my menagerie through breeding or by acquiring at a pet store, the emptiness of my heart continued to grow colossal in size. And yet, though the sometimes overwhelming smells from the animals mingled with the high humidity created from the constantly bubbling aquariums to create a potent witches' brew, I loved it. In all honesty, however, I also contributed to the barnyard-like smell of my room due to a horrific bedwetting problem that lingered throughout childhood and into my early adult life.

Interestingly, the apple doesn't fall far from the tree. My nine-year-old daughter would accumulate animals like me if we let her. Though we have a family dog, chickens, canary, and she has a pair of breeding hamsters and a fish in her room, it is still necessary to reign in her own animal collecting tendencies that could easily veer into hoarding territory. One way we have let her have a positive outlet is to allow her to breed hamsters, because we discovered that it is impossible to obtain teddy bear hamsters at any pet store in our city of Duluth. We feel it is a safe bet that she will be able to sell these cuddly hamsters that have been tamed under her watchful care, and this way they won't multiply into uncontrollable numbers. Her observing of the animals mating, the rapid pregnancy that lasts just two weeks, and the delivery and development of the offspring, is turning out to be a rewarding experience for her. In fact, almost immediately after writing this, my wife came down the stairs and said she could watch the hamsters all day. The litter of 10 babies is now about 15 days old, and their eyes are starting to open. The restless creatures are beginning to wander around the cage. Stumbling upon solid food for the first time, they partake. These are wonderful experiences for anyone to enjoy in the right quantities.

5

CURLY

I rescued him from the kill room of a local animal shelter. I was five years old, and still adjusting to my parents' divorce. Mom wisely decided that I needed a dog. Curly was my most consistent and steady friend while growing up. My only brother. Thus, he gets his own chapter.

We visited several shelters, and being unreasonably picky, I couldn't find one I liked. Finally, at the last shelter, they brought us into a room containing their least desirables that had been around too long.

Curly was crammed into a tiny cage so small that he couldn't turn around. The poodle's filthy white fur was grown out and knotted in a cross between a full-bodied Afro and dreadlocks. Our eyes made contact, he moaned a little, and I wanted to take him home instantly. This must have been the happiest dog on earth when he arrived at our house. I played ball with him in the kitchen for hours. We became best friends instantly. In those days there was room on the kitchen floor to throw a ball and for the dog to retrieve it while sliding around on the floor at full speed, crashing into the wall.

Throughout my childhood until he died when I was away at my freshman year of college, he perfectly filled the roles of best friend and brother. On February 11, 1995, I received a horrible phone call from my mom, "I just thought I'd call and tell you that Curly died last night." The news hit me like a ton of bricks. It felt as if a vital organ had been torn from my body. I was despondent, depressed, and unable to attend most classes for a week. I sank into a significant depression in the weeks that followed, feeling lonely as ever while I questioned whether any of the friendships I had made in college were real. Curly was one of the few constants in my life. I felt like I had lost a brother. I had no other siblings. He was always home and available. Whenever I sat home alone watching television, Curly usually snuggled up next to me.

Of course, he could also be a gigantic pain in the ass. As mentioned, his excrement and urine polluted every room of the house. Upon entering the house, we immediately encountered the stench of his waste products mingled along with mold, rotting food, dust, despair, and poverty. My best friend's excitement to see me was wonderful to return home to, however. Arriving alone after a long day at school, I turned the key in the lock. The vacuum seal of the house broke as foul gases rushed into the void of the world's atmosphere. As my lungs filled and acclimated to the stench, a process somewhat like drowning, Curly and I playfully embraced while feeling safe in one another's arms. Frequently I wept violently as he eagerly drank my salty tears.

He peed on my school shoes more than once. During one particularly memorable instance, I failed to realize this until I was stepping on the bus bound for school. I was in seventh grade, feeling plenty awkward on a good day. Incredibly foul-smelling shoes certainly didn't add to my social standing. The olfactory receptors of anyone within 10 feet of me went on overload. Several long quizzical stares were sent in my direction. The day dragged on interminably. The clock seemed to move in reverse.

On three or four occasions, he violently bit me in the face when I wouldn't leave him alone following a warning growl. These episodes left me with significant puncture wounds and large scabs that invited questions and stares from onlookers. At the time I was shocked and fascinated by the amount of power the 15-pound dog possessed in his rapidly compressing jaws. In the span of a second or two I sustained several devastating bites to the kisser. Curly followed this up with tender licks and a contrite heart. The wild was never fully removed from him, which was also one of his redeeming qualities.

It wasn't unusual for him to be left alone to roam the house for eight or more hours every day. The idea of kenneling him up wasn't even dreamed of. Of course, he tore into things on a daily basis. If we forgot to cover and weigh down the large garbage can in the kitchen, which was perhaps a size of 35 gallons or more and took large black garbage bags, he tipped over the contents. We arrived home to find smelly wet trash covering the open floor space in the kitchen, living room, and even into the distant hallway that led to our bedrooms. Sometimes the debris even made the long migration into our beds. Mom and I were displeased, but we knew it was our own fault for leaving him alone for hours on end. If Mom's on-again, off-again boyfriend of 35 years, Enoch, happened to be with us, he would be enraged to the point that I feared for Curly's life. His most common punishment for the dog, after we had cleaned all the sloppy goop up, was to drop the dog right into the slimy garbage can. He was left there to learn his lesson for an hour or so. I was forbidden from providing succor or relief of any kind. Curly did have his own techniques of defiance and retribution, however.

Now one of the first things Enoch did after arriving unannounced and abruptly opening the door by kicking it past the sticky spot with the point of his boot, was lie down on the couch and have me pull those smelly cowboy boots off. In those early days while I was young, the first of the two couches was often clean enough to allow a man to recline as such. My task involved a few loosening wiggles before the boot would satisfyingly slide off from the shins to the ankle, and then required an upward tip to remove them from his now liberated feet. As his sweaty socks aired out some of their wretched gaminess, I set his boots out of the way in the hall. Now it was time to deal with the dreaded stockings. They were long, dark blue, pulled up high, and moist. Peeling them off like a banana peel revealed sore, puffy, white and pinkish feet riddled with toe-jam. After the majority of offending fluff was removed, I worked a plentiful supply of yellow moisturizing lotion in and around all crevices and creases of his feet and ankles. I diligently smeared it between all 10 toes while working it in everywhere. As the man laid back with his eyes closed, giving an occasional sigh of satisfaction, Curly lifted his left leg up high and shot a perfect arc of urine high up and into the boots. It was a direct hit, and Mom and I laughed hysterically.

Often when Enoch arrived on a Friday evening he scooped us up like baby chicks from our nest. Completely against my will and without any warning, he took us to his home in a rough neighborhood of Milwaukee. Each of those weekends seemed like the longest days of my life. Coming smack dab between unrelenting weeks with the babysitter, they were pretty much Hell on earth.

Curly, apparently feeling the same way and needing a little action, shot out the front door like a nothing-to-lose escapee. On one occasion, I chased him out the door and into the foreign neighborhood, beginning an epic hour-long chase. Running right down the middle of the street at full bore, Curly was out-of control and had lost all inhibition. A large moving truck thundered toward us from the opposite direction, and I was certain my only comfort was doomed to become a speed bump in the pavement. No amount of screaming caused my dog to turn back or veer from his current course. Through a sheer miracle, and due to his short height, he kept a straight line while running under the truck. The driver maintained his full speed the entire time, and Curly passed between the wheels completely unharmed and unaware of how he nearly lost his life. My panic seemed to near the point of a heart attack, but the saga was only beginning.

I nearly lost sight of the dog on several occasions. If I had I'm convinced he would have been lost forever. He led our rabbit chase through an increasingly rough and violent neighborhood. A gang hanging out on a street corner sent some teasing jeers my way, drunks occasionally shuffled along the cracked sidewalk in the middle of the day, and I slowed some while running past a disheveled person pushing a shopping cart full of recyclables. At the climax of our adrenaline-fueled chase, Curly mindlessly darted across a frighteningly busy four-lane road, which took me considerable time to safely jaywalk across. Finally, I nabbed the dog as he sniffed a wrapper that had blown into a chain-link fence at the edge of a shopping center parking lot that resembled a wasteland. Sweaty and exhausted, but finally feeling relieved that the drama was over, I held Curly tight in my arms as we struggled to find our way back to the house by retracing our winding steps over the mile or two through the unknown, mysterious city. This was more than I could reasonably handle at the age of 10. Survival instincts kicked in, however, and we made it back. On the bright side, it is one of my favorite stories.

6

CADDY VISTA

My neighborhood, Caddy Vista, was situated at the extreme northern end of Racine County a stone's throw from Milwaukee County. The subdivision of homes was plopped down between cornfields back in the post-war era of the 1950's as demand for affordable housing stock was increasing. All 200 dwellings were virtually identical in the Levittown style, having been built in a factory and set down on concrete slabs within their individual lots. Being a significant distance from both cities of Racine and Milwaukee, our development didn't seem to fall under either's orbit or fit in anywhere. We were in the country, but this wasn't country living.

The three bedroom houses are rather peculiar, containing no basement or attic. They do, however, boast a utility/laundry room, and have a small cubbyhole in the back of the house to access the plumbing. Our water heater was in the kitchen, and a three-foot-long pipe carried hot water to the bathroom through this small space. These houses are a plumber's dream.

Caddy Vista was a development targeted for low-income families, and all the usual problems and family dysfunctions thrived in our neighborhood. Wealthier enclaves have their own issues, but these are not nearly as visible as they are among the very poor. Child abuse, drug use, alcoholism, neglect, derelict homes, and extreme bullying, were common. And yet, there were a few individuals who were considered wealthy and owned corvettes, classic cars, or took pride in their homes.

For two years, starting at age 12, I was responsible for a paper route that took me right through the heart of Caddy Vista. By and large, this was a positive experience that instilled a solid work ethic. I delivered the Milwaukee Journal six afternoons a week. The monstrous Sunday morning paper required waking no later than 4:00 am so I could assemble the three-inch-thick newspaper, and then pull my wagon nearly a mile mostly uphill to start my route. Throughout most of my tenure I used a red Radio Flyer wagon from when I was a little kid, stretching long bungee cords to keep the papers in place. Occasionally this resulted in disaster, such as on New Year's Day in 1989, which was bitterly cold, windy, and icy. My overloaded wagon tipped over, resulting in most of the ads and inserts blowing across a wide area. Shortly after this I obtained a tall wagon with large sides made of plywood from a former paperboy. This wagon was then pushed throughout my route, requiring considerable effort, but without the stress of constantly adjusting the ever-shifting papers. The job provided tremendous exercise. I'd return home after running through most of the route, and my legs gave a satisfying twitching feeling as I reclined on the couch before most people had even arisen. It was an incredible amount of work for the sake of around $20 profit each week. Commanding no allowance, however, the income opened up many opportunities for me to squander money on baseball cards and pets.

One of my customers, Ms. Whitney, was an ancient elderly lady. She was the sweetest thing ever. Standing somewhere around 50 inches tall, and possessing an unusually high voice, Ms. Whitney cast an appearance akin to an extremely aged Little Red Riding Hood. Collecting the $2.50 from her each week was an exercise in patience. It frequently took her ten minutes to reach the door, the exertion of crossing the tiny house being so great. Our short conversations were probably the highlight of her day or week. I always felt a special kinship with her. She treated me kindly, and was also a hoarder. The piles in her living room were neatly arranged to a steady height about waist-high. Her paths cut a neat 90-degree angle through her possessions in a city-like grid format. Once she had me wait an interminable period of time as she retrieved my picture honoring me in the paper as the Milwaukee Journal's carrier of the week, which she had thoughtfully framed for me.

My first real friend in the world was named Eddie. He lived directly across the circular cul-de-sac that we shared, which we used endlessly for playing kickball, baseball, and riding Big Wheels and bikes. We shared both joy and misery together. While his home was much cleaner than mine, I always felt sorry for him. His parents were about as mean and ignorant as trolls.

Fast-forwarding about 20 years, just to shade things in a bit
for you, his mom died of a heroin overdose on the couch in
my old living room. Following her last divorce, she lived in
near-prostitution for the better part of a decade in order to
have a place to lay her head. Mom allowed her to live rent-
free in our hovel of a home for a couple years. This was a
decade or so after I had moved out at the age of 18. Then, as
now, Mom was attempting to find a way to get out from
under this albatross of a house by taking a job in another part
of the state. While she lived in an apartment the old house
went unused. She would have sold it in a flash, but since it
was full of her things this was not possible. The same problem
continues to manifest itself today, and is a matter of constant
conversation.

Unfortunately, Eddie's mother mined the house for anything
of value that could be pawned for drug money, such as my
great-grandmother's old jewelry. She also committed identity
theft, taking advantage of my mom's complete lack of
organization. Things like her social security card and bank
statements were randomly lying at the bottoms of piles
throughout the house, and continue to do so. I found my own
original birth certificate during one recent cleanout along
with other important papers containing my social security
number, all entombed within a mountain of debris.

My mother meant well in coming to her aid, but
unfortunately never has been a good judge of character.
Since she doesn't keep track of anything very well, she didn't
think twice when she stopped receiving her credit card bills.

In addition to new accounts being opened, the addict also made sure to have the current bills of Mom's existing credit cards go to the house. This way she was able to max out all of Mom's cards while also charging the new cards to their limits as well. This went on for a year or more. To add insult to injury, my mom is the one who discovered the dead body in her living room following the overdose.

At the end of it all, Mom was on the hook for over $40,000. She claims the credit card companies wouldn't write off all the debt due to identity theft since so much time had elapsed. I will probably never know the full story, and remain frustrated that I couldn't help her navigate these treacherous waters. Though her credit score had already been walloped down to the low 200's, she saddled herself with a high-rate mortgage on her house in order to quickly sweep the problem under the rug. She had spent 30 years paying off the $27,000 original purchase price of our house, and the mortgage was now reset at $40,000 in order to pay off charges due to identity theft that I contend she never should have paid. This is a window into endless arguments I have with her. She nearly lost her home due to this situation, and frankly I have fretted that both my parents may lose their homes due to financial stress at some point. I feel ill-equipped mentally, emotionally, and financially, to house them with my family.

Additionally, Eddie's stepdad was an angry alcoholic, so he had two very unstable "parents" to deal with. One afternoon and evening over a span of about 10 hours, my friend and his three little sisters were left in the hands of a teenage girl for a babysitter. She decided to invite her boyfriend, who invited his friends, and before we knew it there were somewhere around 50 hooligans running in and around his house trashing the place. Before they physically chased Eddie and me out of the house with threats, I saw one of them drinking liquor right from a bottle taken from the well-stocked liquor cabinet. After setting the bottle down, the bastard threw my friend's baby sister high into the air repeatedly as she screamed in terror. The party raged on for hours into the dark. This was before the age of 911 in our community. My mom was gone, and all the neighbors I was familiar with had vanished as well.

Eventually scary old Gus came home. He lived immediately next to the action. This was a very large man with long unkempt hair, a huge boiler of a belly with its enormous belly button usually exposed, and he hardly ever wore a smile. He was perhaps 40 years old at the time, still lived with his mother, and his house smelled nearly as bad as mine. Oddly enough, I remember many men like him in our neighborhood. I scarcely can recall any male role models.

While Eddie and I huddled in the ditch—afraid to be seen—yelling, screaming, panic, and mass chaos dramatically unfurled. All of a sudden dozens of teenagers bolted out of both doors of the house like hornets flying out of a hive just kicked. Gus yelled at the top of his lungs and single-handedly chased them all out. Barefoot and bare-chested, all he had on was an old pair of jeans, reminiscent of the Incredible Hulk. A scary sight indeed. No doubt the memory remains seared into everyone's minds.

As you can see, Eddie and I went through a lot together. We lived with constant drama. We relied on each other to not only survive, but we also thrived as friends collecting baseball cards, dreaming of playing major league baseball, and just being normal kids. One day, upon returning home from school on the bus, an acquaintance said that Eddie's home had been foreclosed and that his house had been packed up that very day. Of course I didn't believe it. Best friends don't just up and move without warning. Besides, I had just hung out with him the day before. Sadly, I ran to his house and discovered it was true.

The home was completely empty. All that remained as evidence that my buddy had once lived there were several of his baseball cards strewn all over the floor. His family had been evicted. The entire house was packed up while Eddie was at school. He apparently was picked up from his private school (paid for by his real dad), after what was no doubt an ordinary day, only to learn of the horrible truth as he was driven to a motel they were to live in for months. We were both in 6th grade at the time. That was pretty much the last I heard of him other than a couple of awkward meetings about 10 years later. Crazy. I would never want to convey that my childhood was as difficult as his must have been. Unlike Eddie, I had a mother that cared for me as best she knew how.

Steve, my next friend, took Eddie's place for several years. He lived a mile away in a small oasis of a neighborhood. He and his family looked down on our crappy little community (as nearly everyone did). His dad owned a successful lumberyard. Most people today would call them middle class, but I thought of them as spectacularly rich because they bought brand new cars and had a nice concrete driveway.

They always ate great food, were well dressed, and obviously didn't worry about money. We built elaborate forts in his woods that survived the winter, spent hours cutting large branches high up in my willow trees just to see them fall, burned these branches in enormous bonfires after they dried, went on our first long bike rides away from home into the city together, and talked about girls.

Sometimes Mom even dropped us off at the nearest bus stop in Milwaukee County 10 miles away. From there we'd end up making four to five bus connections in order to get to County Stadium to see the Milwaukee Brewers play baseball. These were fantastic experiences. Being the comparative micro-manager that I am now I would certainly not let my kids do this, but my horizons were broadened immensely. This was long before the era of ubiquitous cell phones. We were 100% independent on these epic journeys that lasted hours.

We stayed at the ballpark late into the night, waiting at the players' entrance in order to obtain autographs from the players as they walked out to their cars after the game. I still cherish my Rawlings baseball glove that is loaded with numerous obscure players that took the time to sign it after the game, and a few luminaries as well. Head cases like Gary Sheffield always walked right past us without saying a word, but we enjoyed seeing the fancy sports cars in which many of the guys drove off. I recall Sheffield having a particularly ostentatious ride that was entirely black, windows included, and spotlessly clean, with gold rims. We also pestered the visiting team if we happened upon them waiting in their bus. We had particular success doing this with the Minnesota

Twins, and handed our gloves up to the players that had nothing else to do while waiting anyway. The signatures of Dan Gladden, Kent Hrbek, and Kirby Puckett, were obtained on the same day. Still gracing my baseball glove, these names mean more to me now that I live in Minnesota.

Somehow we always got home safely in the middle of the night on the latest available bus. This was crucial. It wouldn't have been a good idea to be stranded in a rough part of town without bus service. These were grand adventures for us at the age of 12 - 13 years old, and we were fortunate enough to attend 20 - 25 games a year, mostly without any supervision.

Unfortunately Steve abandoned me at a time when I made an embarrassing spectacle of myself by cutting off my eyebrows at the beginning of our freshman year of high school. One looks quite odd with wild hair and no eyebrows. There will be more to come on that later. Our friendship never recovered, and this was a particularly difficult time for me.

7

ALONE WITH NIGHTMARES AND CREEPY CRAWLIES

The crushing, all-consuming, intensity of my loneliness was palpable. I feared it as though it stalked me, when really it emanated from an emptiness within. My first knowledge of it came when I was six years old. I had a nightmare, and went to my mom's room for comfort. She was gone. Vanished! I frantically searched every room of the house, crying out for her, to no avail. I went to sleep in her bed, snuggled up among a pillow and blankets, and cried myself to sleep. It turned out that she had gone to a bar. Naturally, she needed others too.

From then on she let me know ahead of time when she was going out, and allowed me to sleep in her bed on those evenings once or twice a week. One night, while sleeping alone in her room that faced the circular cul-de-sac out front, I had a nightmare that it was World War III. An atomic bomb detonating in the distance violently shook me from my slumber. I woke up in a startled fright, only to realize it wasn't a dream! The bright white flash was positively blinding as it fully illuminated the room with its piercing light. My panic reached near hysteria as I awaited the flesh-stripping force of the blast. Finally, the car that had lit my mother's room with its headlights completed its orbit around the circle.

Interestingly, this paranoia revisited me during my freshman year of college. I had fallen asleep in the front row during my most boring class, calculus. I dreamed a similarly vivid dream complete with the sound of the bomb going off. I awoke bolt upright in a hot sweat to the roar of some fighter jets that had apparently made a pass fairly close to the school. I let out a full scream that brought chuckles throughout the entire lecture hall of perhaps 80 - 100 students.

Loneliness, boredom, self-loathing, and a complete lack of direction marked the five long years spent at my babysitter's house that did not end until the day I entered sixth grade. Summer was particularly dreary and awful. Every day the three girls and I were expected to stay outside the entire day in the heat, while the babysitter's son was allowed to stay inside with the air conditioning, watching television. Remaining in her yard virtually the entire time in utter boredom, I took to playing with ants and observing as much of the natural world as I could in the small yard. A large anthill teemed with a bustling civilization along the far narrow side of the house, where I enjoyed relative privacy. I fed worms and other bugs to the ants, watching them struggle for hours to push, pull, and drag their prey underground. I rarely disturbed them in any way, but simply studied their comings and goings. I also followed the workers as they ventured out on hunts or exploratory missions. Occasionally I introduced a red ant or two in order to watch the fighting that ensued. The black ants overwhelmed them in large numbers as they thundered out of the nest shouting, "For queen and colony!"

Once at this same location, several neighborhood bullies laid me down on top of this very anthill with two girls holding my hands down. They took turns taking running blows into my stomach as my body smashed back into the wall of the house, thus causing my stomach to take the full brunt of dozens of punches and kicks. Finally they relented, leaving me for the ants to haul down into deep caverns to sustain their brood like any other piece of meat. Eventually I stumbled to the front door doubled over in agony, barely able to breathe. I am at a loss as to why I chose to take their punishment rather than fight back, yell, or struggle to round the corner to the relative safety of the front yard. The capacity of the abused to remain silent and take what's coming to them can be limitless. Upon repeated questioning I chose not to get anyone in trouble. Additionally, I never once told Mom about this instance or how awful it was in this babysitter's care. I was convinced it would have made matters worse. If only I had spoken up, things may have changed.

During a crisis I was marooned in isolation, and found ways to grind through as best I could. At one point a large brute was hell-bent on beating me up, even though he was a junior or senior in high school and I was still in seventh grade. This was due to a slip-of-the-tongue at the bus stop, which was quickly passed on to him. There was nobody to discuss options with. This was one of many epic gut-wrenching imbroglios I confronted with seemingly no solution. I tried calling the police, but they calmly informed me that they were unable to assist if I didn't provide the bully's name. Somehow I managed to avoid his pounding fists for three terrifying weeks.

One day I trundled down the steps of the bus with my fully loaded backpack and a trumpet in an awkward case. Immediately after the safety of the bus slipped away, the giant stepped out from the shadows. He was wearing nothing but a pair of spandex shorts. Smoking a cigarette, sporting facial hair, and well-cut muscles, the hulk cast an appearance of a grown man rather than that of a mere boy. Amidst the delighted screams of his girlfriend, "Get him Corey! Kick his ass," he calmly extinguished his cigarette prior to taking care of business. I have never felt so helpless or scared in my life, and that's saying something. I was still somewhere in the neighborhood of 85 pounds, short, and timid. Adrenaline kicked in, and I ran like never before. Keep in mind that the bully had nothing on but essentially a partial tracksuit, while I was weighed down by a backpack full of books and a large musical instrument case. Shooting ahead with all my might 300 yards to the first corner, I glanced behind to see him in a full sprint behind me. This is the terror an antelope feels with a lion in hot pursuit.

In sheer agony and helplessness I cried out, "God help me!" As the trumpet case banged against my right leg, the latch came undone and the trumpet fell out onto the ground. Somehow I was able to stop to rescue it from inevitable destruction while still avoiding the pounding. I managed to outrun the stronger boy the full 600 yards to my house, and still believe that I was carried on the wings of eagles. This was like the Red Sea being parted for the Israelites as they escaped a well-equipped Egyptian army.

The weeks dragged on. All day long at school I plotted strategies that allowed me to live another day. I exited the bus in other places, but he wised up to that by following the bus on his bicycle. I resorted to going home with other friends who often were little more than acquaintances, and successfully avoided his punches until he gave up. This was a miracle. Finally, he came into the circle in front of my home and called a truce that I happily accepted.

As my capacity grew for observing other families and the friendships they experienced, I increasingly felt forlornly abandoned in a world of confusion. The sense of isolation swelled like an engorged tick, placing me into solitary confinement so striking that it was as if there was only one small window with bars high above me letting in the sounds of happy fun-loving kids frolicking on a nearby playground that may as well have been on another planet. It was for this reason that I became so addicted to television as a child, and hoarded dozens of pets.

The vast landscape among the world of the humans was nearly bereft of role models to aid in discovering societal norms or standards of hygiene. Usually I learned through trial and error. I already spoke of the situation of not wearing underwear. I inadvertently exposed myself a few times before wising up to the practice. Even with full-length overalls, one must be careful. Go figure, huh? My hair was unkempt. It poofed out, was wild and crazy, and sometimes people taunted me for having head lice as I scratched repeatedly with both hands from front to back. I am pretty sure that I did have lice occasionally, but somehow they must have gone away. I was never treated for it.

My mom was humiliated during a trip to the dentist one year. The hygienist took one scrape with the cleaner pick, and pulled off a shocking amount of gunky white plaque. It had been over a month since I had brushed my teeth, and I never flossed throughout childhood. She proceeded to give Mom quite a lecture on the importance of oral hygiene. Unfortunately I am still paying for those poor choices today, because fillings typically only last 20 years or so.

It took me more than two decades to catch on to the amazing power of soap. In college I started out each year with a free bar or two. When these disappeared I didn't see the need to replace them, because of the amazing clean feeling I got for free while camping by simply jumping into a lake. I did use shampoo, but soap on the body seemed unnecessary when clean water washed off any visible dirt. I failed to purchase any soap until my senior year, when my friend Brandon told me that I did indeed stink sometimes. While watching him unpack his groceries one day, I expressed surprise that he wasted his money on soap. "I don't use the stuff, and I don't stink," I told him. His quick surprised retort was, "Sometimes you do!" I was shocked. He sent me on my way with a pure white bar of soap. I have kept a steady supply of this miraculous lathering agent on hand ever since.

8

BEDWETTING AND ALL THAT JAZZ

I am quite confident that I had some of the most disgusting bed sheets on the planet, and possibly in the known universe. I was beset by a horrendous bedwetting problem that set me apart from my peers. It didn't disappear entirely until my freshman year of college, which was itself marked by a few accidents early on. Thus, I can forever claim the distinction of having remained a bedwetter into the dawn of adulthood. Perhaps my recovery from this humiliating condition should become a selling point on my resume. It is displayed prominently on my business card at any rate.

Frankly, due to my own struggles that lasted the better part of two decades, I am shocked that my own kids haven't had to wrestle with a monstrous bedwetting problem at all. Their total accumulation of accidents, which occurred at the tender ages of four and five, likely didn't surpass what I had to deal with during challenging weeks in middle or high school.

Every day that started out dry and clean was cause to celebrate. I still occasionally woke in the middle of the night covered in urine from major lake-like accidents while in 12th grade. On the small number of occasions that I slept somewhere else around other people, I was highly vigilant in dehydrating myself by mid-afternoon the day before. Usually this worked, but occasionally my touchy bladder thwarted my best efforts. While staying with my grandparents they would wake me to "go" in the middle of the night, and I invariably became an irrational mess. Screaming at the top of my lungs while kicking and punching, bracing myself between every passing doorway as I was forcibly carried to the bathroom, these were raging battles that could last the better part of an hour. In the morning I woke up as the sweet little grandson with no recollection of the goings on from the night before, but I do have a few memories of being peeled away from doorframes. The two or three occasions that I moistened the sheets in a bedroom at someone else's house, found me up at 4:00 in the morning frantically deploying desperate countermeasures. If I couldn't find identical sheets and a clothes hamper to sneak the dirty ones into, I sat there for hours aiming a fan at the bed with the window open even on cold days. Somehow I escaped these situations without any embarrassing comments being directed my way, although I have to believe the parents whispered about it later.

My plumbing also seemed to sense strategically inconvenient times for an accident that offered up the most potential for life-altering outcomes. I became a master at calmly covering the situation up nonchalantly. The following disasters illustrate this perfectly.

During the summer following my sophomore or junior year, I embarked upon my first ever backpacking trip. The Wisconsin Walkabout was a 100-mile hike in the Kettle Moraine State Forest over a ten-day span—more importantly, there were ten nights to fret over and micromanage—with approximately 15 other high schoolers from my school district. Though it was located only an hour away from home near the northern suburbs of Milwaukee, it seemed like a bountiful wilderness paradise. I had accidents on just two of those ten evenings, but each called for a take-no-chances approach for complete resolution. After all, there were cute girls I liked on this trip.

The first incident involved a simple dampening of the entire front of my whitey tighties, a shot across the bow if you will. That was no big deal for a pro like me. I simply woke up before dawn, changed my undies out in the woods after a brutally cold scrubbing of my vitals with frigid water, and then either threw the pair that had successfully acted as a sponge down an outdoor latrine, or buried them far away under some leaves. I have used both methods depending on the circumstances, so it is impossible for me to verify for the inquisitive reader which option was employed here. Crawling back into my sleeping bag I woke up hours later in a normal condition like everyone else.

The last night of the trip was not so easy to deal with. Bear in mind that I had made it through nine consecutive evenings largely unscathed. I was feeling pretty good about myself. This night it was very cold with temperatures dipping down into the lower 30's, so I slept with my only pair of blue jeans on for warmth. Of course, the dam completely failed on this particular evening. Every last ounce of moisture passed through the floodgates, threatening to wash away any shred of dignity that remained intact. Both me and my sleeping bag were thoroughly drenched with urine. In my memory it remains reminiscent, in terms of quantity, of seeing an elephant at the zoo expelling two gallons per second as a 42-gallon-capacity bladder emptied before the eyes of my children in what was certainly the high point of our day there, lest I digress. This was a desperate situation indeed.

The underwear was thoroughly soaked, a lost cause, and the entire front of my jeans were drenched down to my knees. The cotton fibers of my t-shirt AND sweatshirt also wicked up plenty of moisture in what was apparently a complete lapse in my usual dehydration defense, likely brought on by needing plenty of water following a day filled with exertion.

I dealt with the crisis in the wee hours as I had earlier, but this time I was forced to wear a small pair of nylon shorts along with my last pair of bright, white, clean briefs. In the morning, while everyone was shivering and bundled up in their warmest clothes, I casually stood around in a pair of shorts as if I was perfectly comfortable and relaxed. Even though my skinny chicken legs betrayed me by turning a purplish color with goose bumps all over them, I had to lie and say I felt fine when everyone asked why I didn't just put on pants. I was standing in the presence of a large group of my peers, mostly girls, and there was no other option but to work with what I had. I simply didn't have a dry pair of pants to enjoy, which was impossible to explain because everyone saw me in jeans the night before.

The worst experience of all came as a sort of grand finale. It was on the morning of the Wisconsin state cross country meet in Wisconsin Rapids during my senior year. Our team stayed in a hotel, and was one of the top contenders in the state. Since I had forgotten a spare pair of underwear, fate seemed to dictate that I would have an out-of-control fire-hose-style gusher in the middle of this night. My only hope was to douse the entire front of my Fruit of the Looms with borrowed cologne from my roommate.

Incidentally, this was the only time I ever told someone about an emergency like this. I made the exception in order to obtain the powerful fragrance as a cover-up, and also because Ryan Silich was different from anyone else on our team. While he wasn't a close friend, he was completely trustworthy. He was a Christian, and one of the only people I ever encountered throughout childhood, if not the only one, who lived a life that matched the religious beliefs he espoused. Ryan was generally considered relatively corny and straight-laced, which was a stereotype I went through great pains to avoid. Everyone respected him, however, even as they held their distance.

After the trauma was dealt with, I ran the 5k race with moist skivvies underneath thin nylon shorts. It was a bitterly cold morning with snow on the ground, high winds, and below freezing temperatures. I was profoundly uncomfortable, didn't run my best race, but at least the crisis was averted in that my secret was not discovered among a group of guys that would have quickly dispersed embarrassing information like this throughout the school. That would have been the end of the world! Needless to say, it was highly irritating to the skin to be confined to those defiled undergarments all through the day and for the long drive home that lasted several hours. Shame bottled up under pressure, with no possibility of an outlet. My sense of desolation and lack of purpose culminated the next day in an encounter with a locomotive that nearly ended my life.

Even on a good, clean, dry day at home, my sheets remained incredibly filthy. They reflected the general state of my room, house, and life. I failed to change the linens for months on end. I simply rotated my position on the large full-sized bed. I contorted into unusual angles, as if playing the game Twister, in an effort to avoid the yellow stains. The location of my head on the bed varied among every conceivable location and direction.

As previously referenced, the space between the sheets and blankets also were littered with sharply jagged empty seed hulls from the birds, and hardened droppings that disintegrated into dust over time. As I moved around in bed I could feel all these oddly shaped, cutting, scratchy, projectiles rubbing up on me all over. It is crazy to think of it now, but at the time it only seemed odd when I occasionally saw how absolutely pristine the rooms of other kids looked compared to mine. I'd lay quietly in bed crying out in my mind and heart to be delivered. A calming presence and an awareness of protection frequently stilled my anxiety. As ridiculously pretentious as it may sound, I firmly believe that the Almighty was guarding my vulnerable spirit in a special way.

9

RAGING ENOCH

"YOU WANNA GET SHOT!? JOANN, GET THE GUN!"

It is remarkable how this verbatim statement is emblematic of our relationship with Enoch. The man, Mom's on-and-off boyfriend of nearly 35 years, bruised through life as an intimidator, enlisting her as an assistant in his war with the world.

Careening through Milwaukee at breakneck speed, we were en route to yet another weekend at his house. The line of demarcation between a relatively peaceful evening alone with Mom and being sucked into a black hole with Enoch as the center of gravity was always as sudden and traumatic as an abduction. Enjoying a Friday evening alone with Mom after a hellacious week at the babysitter's, by 6:30 p.m. I began to entertain the fantasy of an entire weekend devoid of his all-consuming presence while relishing the prospect of fun quality time with her and my friend Eddie. Inevitably, with a kick of the boot and a sudden loud opening of the front door, he barged in unannounced to take us back with him. I was rarely made aware in advance of these plans, and was expected to pick up and leave at a moment's notice.

I had successfully extracted a promise from Mom to stop this practice just days before this particular occasion. That Saturday I went with her to a flea market feeling good about the weekend. While this wasn't my number one idea of fun, I was excited to just be with Mom. For those of you that aren't junk collectors, and possibly not in the know, a flea market isn't a market for fleas. Although, speaking from experience, they sometimes will flourish in the homes of those who frequent them. The larger ones are like gigantic rummage sales with people selling odd junk, old Tupperware, tools, etc, in various booths lined up into infinity. Across the sea of people and tables of wares, I caught a glimpse of Enoch watching us in the distance through his tinted glasses. Immediately crestfallen I turned to Mom exclaiming, "But you promised!" Her response was one of odd befuddlement, as if I had uttered a nonsensical statement. Shrugging her shoulders, she simply said, "So?" Though I was very young, the memory remains vivid as a turning point in our relationship.

From this very moment I learned I could not trust her word. Sadly, though I still love her, this is still the case. It wasn't the breaking of the promise that hurt me, but rather the absolute indifference to having done so. If she had been apologetic, or made some sort of deal with me, I could have deflected this heart-penetrating harpoon. I have since learned that compulsive lying and hoarding frequently go together like peas and carrots. I could try to understand it, but I frankly don't have the energy when I know I'm powerless to restore her to wholeness. There is a potent mix of psychological disorders going on that demand treatment. These are way beyond my pay grade. Thus far I have been unable to convince her to seek the help she needs.

Anyhow, there I was stewing in the back of Enoch's small Dodge Colt hatchback car, which was somewhat akin to earlier versions of the Ford Fiesta or the Omni. Though it was just a four-cylinder garbage can on wheels, he was immensely proud of what it could do on the road, because it had a turbo-enhanced engine. He zipped down the freeway as if competing in the Daytona 500 at high speeds mastering all three lanes. When someone got in his way he made sure to let them know, even though this was one of the smallest cars on the road. Apparently in this particular case the other driver, in a sports car that could have done well in a police chase, wasn't at all intimidated. He certainly had issues of his own, and zoomed out in front of us and blocked us in alongside a semi-truck. By the time our vehicle escaped, tempers in both vehicles reached nuclear-meltdown status. Over the course of several minutes, which seemed to stretch into eternity, both cars raced alongside and chased each other through fairly heavy traffic at speeds reaching 90 miles per hour.

Eventually Enoch was successful at pulling up alongside the muscle car, as we shot down the freeway like twin rockets. He had my mom roll her window down so he could shout at the opposing driver. They both hollered at each other while also occasionally glancing at traffic to avoid a high-speed multiple-car pileup that certainly would have killed us all. More than once he glanced up to find a slow truck traveling at an easy 45 to 50 mph. Slamming on the brakes violently, we then had to step on it to catch back up and continue the argument. Ultimately, after repeated attempts at winning the argument were rebuffed, Enoch irrationally hollered at the carbon copy of himself in the other car, "YOU WANNA GET SHOT!? JOANN, GET THE GUN!"

At this point Mom clumsily fumbled around in the glove compartment using her best deadpan face as if they engaged in this sort of activity all the time. Unwilling to go this far up the crazy scale, the other vehicle finally backed off. Enoch won the argument, got the upper hand, and this was of paramount importance. When he committed to a matter of contention he was all in.

Keep in mind that an eight-year-old child sat terrified and frozen in the back seat. When I could no longer remain silent during the episode, I had begged for mercy. Mom failed to serve as my advocate. She shouted, "EDDY, SHUT UP!"

The main problem with drivers like this is that they seem to have no knowledge that their actions can result in the deaths or serious injuries of other people. To this day I cannot ride in the back seat of a car comfortably, and am barely able to ride as a passenger at all. I am literally terrified of busy city traffic if the driver isn't calmly driving 55 miles per hour and staying in one lane. Any encroachment on an adequate following distance—rigidly defined as a minimum of two seconds of travel time behind the car being tailed, which I periodically count while approaching a mile marker—or lane switching during busy traffic produces extreme anxiety and causes me to clench the arm rest as if I'm passing a kidney stone. For this reason, when forced to use the automobile, I need to engage in nearly all the driving. On long trips, if I fall asleep in the passenger seat I wake up in mere moments screaming from a nightmarish crash occurring in my mind. This is rather alarming for the other passengers, some of whom are jolted violently out of their slumber by my outburst.

If it were up to me, our family would go car-free in a heartbeat. I prefer the bike to the car any day of the week, and would happily invest in a pedicab to tote tired family members around if necessary. With the occasional rental car, a physically fit and adventurous family could thrive with such a lifestyle. Sadly, my wife and kids disagree. For some reason they think the notion is ridiculous given that we live in a climate where ice, snow, and frigid temperatures can persist six months out of the year. Go figure. We have been able to thrive as a one-car family, however, so I have at least been able to savor the reduction of stress from two cars at any rate.

I went through my own period of high-risk driving, which we'll get to at some point, but I have since grown into a slow Toyota Prius driver who cautiously minds the speed limit while watching the gas mileage carefully. Living in a small city suits me. Even passing through a large city causes my anxiety and stress to heighten to the point that the journey is nearly rendered untenable. The aggression and recklessness are more than I can handle. I attribute this to multiple experiences in the back seat of Enoch's car. The man is plenty combative and intimidating with two feet firmly planted on the ground, but get him behind the wheel and these traits amplify exponentially.

I simply cannot get in a car with him again. In college, going back on an earlier resolution not to engage in this risky behavior, I reluctantly buckled in next to him in his big Buick. He was driving me to an auto parts store to generously purchase some car parts for me. It was snowing heavily for Milwaukee's standards, and there were four or five inches of new snow on the road. Seemingly oblivious to the driving conditions, he continued to drive the speed limit while tailing other cars closely. Knowing that any calling into question of his driving abilities was tantamount to questioning his manhood, I silently hyperventilated as a courteous passenger while hoping the danger would pass. When I could no longer withstand the stress, similar to dozens of experiences in childhood, I calmly asked in the sweetest voice possible, "I'm so sorry, but can you slow down a little for me? I realize you're in complete control, and can handle this perfectly, but I am a bit of a wimp of a passenger."

This immediately shot him up to a 10 on the Richter scale for rage. Turning beet red, he shouted at the top of his lungs with veins popping out of his forehead and neck as if he was trying to suck an enormous blueberry through a straw while downing a thick malt. Demonstrating his power over the situation, he sped up to 65 miles per hour on the busy slippery highway while weaving between all lanes and missing the rear bumpers of other cars by mere inches. All I could do was swallow my pride while gently talking him down from the ledge by apologizing profusely and feigning trust in his driving abilities. I always wondered where the police were at these times. Many of these occasions were worthy of arrest. At the very least, an hour spent on the side of the road with a traffic cop would have been intensely gratifying. Amazingly, it never happened. Enoch never did figure out how to secure my mother's hand in marriage. As this incident demonstrates (one of hundreds), he could be generous with his time and money, but rarely treated us with tender kindness.

If you've never pooped in a car, perhaps this story will warm you to the idea. On yet another one of the longest weekends of my life, which they all seemed to be, we were parked at a Mill's Fleet Farm hours from home on the way to the Iola Old Car Show and swap meet during a heat wave at the height of summer. This was a living nightmare when I was six or seven years old. This meant thousands of cars lined up under the hot sun, waiting as he seemed to strike up conversations with every available owner, and a blistering sunburn that painfully lingered for a week.

It was 101 degrees. I know this for a fact, because I couldn't keep myself from watching the bank display that alternated between the temperature and time. Enoch and Mom left me in the car parked in full sun smack dab in the middle of the crowded lot. I was given strict orders not to go anywhere. In fact, Enoch turned around a second time as they departed to the comfortable air conditioning of the store to demand with a pointing finger, "Stay here!"

Time dragged on as if I was stuck in Purgatory. The heat haze emanated in waves from the recently sealed asphalt, which was hot enough to melt the sole of a shoe. The dark

brown car became a greenhouse, within which I rolled my
rear window down for scant relief as I poked my head outside
into the blinding sun. I traced designs in the burgundy
upholstery as the minutes stretched on into longer
increments. A half hour passed. Bored and sweltering, I
opened the door halfway while cautiously planting one foot
onto the blacktop. This provided zero relief. An hour passed
with nothing to do but sweat and dream of a refreshingly cold
soda pop. Dehydrated, and about to swoon, an
uncomfortable pressure began to build in my bowels at about
the 90-minute mark.

The steadily increasing compression of the weighty load
within demanded attention. A fast-food restaurant beckoned
just 100 yards away as an oasis-like mirage. The idea of
enjoying the luxurious climate-controlled restroom of the
seductive Hardee's oasis became a fixation in my
imagination, but I was certain that Enoch would appear at
that exact moment since they were certainly due any time.
Reaching the breaking point I grabbed a newspaper in
desperation, folded it in half, and hovered over it as I
expelled an incredibly lengthy quantity of organic material. I
then pushed the repurposed pages to the space beneath the
driver's seat, hoping it would lie there undiscovered for all
time.

Incredibly, two full weeks went by before I took an angry
phone call from the man. This was July, and the car stank
like he was riding around with a corpse. He had been unable
to find the source of the stench. In near-hysteria he reached
under the car seat one day to discover in horror that the root
of the problem was much worse than he ever dreamed. I

believe the scene also may have involved maggots. A huge argument ensued, which didn't last nearly as long as one might expect. I hollered back that I was ordered not to go anywhere, and that they had been in the store for almost two hours. The two of them had felt some guilt at the time, and in penance bought me a Coca-Cola. After the explanation traced the source of the crime to this incident, there really wasn't much he or my mom could say in response.

Years later at the age of 13 I hit a tipping point. Enoch had left some large pieces of scrap metal and an unfinished homemade garage door opener leaned up along the outside of the garage, which already looked run-down and shoddy. I was responsible for the upkeep of the yard. We didn't own a weed whip, and knee-high weeds graced the exterior wall facing retired neighbors who enjoyed a perfectly manicured lawn. With my friend Steve in the next room, I called Enoch to politely request that he remove these items. Even though I asked in the nicest way possible, his anger and defensiveness soon flew into a rage. He hollered that he'd remove his few things after I cleaned out the garage completely, because I had so much of my own junk in there.

Initially I just sassed back while smiling and showing off for my friend Steve, who was watching. This only served to pour gas on the fire of Enoch's anger. He never backed down from a fight. Ever. Soon the conversation devolved into an eruption of blustering insults. Before long I was crying as we exchanged an unending litany of profanity-laced personal attacks while yelling back-and-forth at the top of our lungs. Emboldened by distance, I screamed, "You worthless lard-ass piece of shit!"

Enoch snapped back, "You're a good-for-nothing kid that'll never amount to anything! You're just like your Dad!" Steve awkwardly stepped outside as the argument raged on in bitter hatred. Following a 45-minute marathon session, feeling as if I had spent a day below ground in a coal mine, I emerged with an agreement from the man to remove his junk if I cleaned the entire garage. Clearly he thought this was impossible.

With some degree of authority I can assert that I had somewhere between 3,000 and 4,000 pounds of newspapers stored in neat rows that reached to a height well above my head. I was a major recycler, and this was years before recycling was cool. I had been collecting newspapers from various homes in the neighborhood for years. It started in third grade after seeing a film in school discussing the problem of excess waste, landfills being filled to capacity, the benefits of recycling, and the like.

Annually my mom shuttled my precious cargo and me to the recycling center in several loads, where it was weighed, and I received a very small payment for the trouble. They were paying $20 per ton at the time, so I doubt this even covered Mom's gas to deliver them. These stacks of papers took up significant space in the garage, and greatly vexed Mom's boyfriend. I had about a year and a half's accumulation of papers stored from a dozen or more homes, and a roadside neighborhood recycling program was beginning in just two weeks. The plan was to recycle them in that manner, but after the offensive phone call I obsessively got to work immediately. I was incapable of backing down from a duel with my nemesis, so with a tinge of guilt we hauled 18 months' worth of newspaper collection to the side of the road to be picked up with the garbage.

The massiveness of the project made this day into one of my favorite childhood memories. We chucked out all the papers, antique furniture, and more detritus than you can imagine. When everything was taken out that could obviously be tossed, we were actually a little disappointed because we had so much momentum, and desired to create the most enormous pile of garbage that the waste haulers had ever seen. We almost certainly succeeded, and ended up ransacking the place in the process. I also had dragged out numerous large black bags filled with junk from the very belly of the beast itself as I scoured every room of the house, and tossed loads of items that were still plenty usable. Draining the swamp of excess stuff was a thrilling experience.

We brought out a few beautiful vintage cane poles that were perhaps ten feet long, affixed homemade flags to them, and jammed them into the pile. Since we wanted to mimic the look of Six Flags Great America as people entered my circular cul-de-sac, we searched high and low for any long poles we could find. By the time we were done the sight was awesome. We beamed with pride. This pile of trash was somewhere on the order of 40 feet wide, six feet deep, and five feet high. Our flags triumphantly reached into the sky above this monument to excess, extending high into the atmosphere. The spectacle was impossible to miss. We had such fun that we laughed like little children all day long. This was an impressive effort for a mere afternoon of unsupervised work. To us it was as if we had constructed the pyramids of Egypt. At about the point we became positively drunk with giddiness, Mom pulled into the driveway with an expression of shock and horror. If only I had a video to document this moment! In today's YouTube-crazed world it would have garnered a million hits or more. Her astonishment, confusion, anger, indecision over what to do, and tension were palpable.

My buddy Steve had begun seeing my house when I was much younger and less self-conscious of its freakishness. Thus, he was grandfathered in to sharing my secret at a relatively late age. This was very cathartic. When he later disappeared from the scene my shame became entirely sealed off and isolated from the rest of humanity.

Garbage day wouldn't arrive for several days, so everyone had to live with our creation for a while. Gradually the creativity of the effort was vandalized to the point that it just became an unsightly mess that resembled a New York City garbage strike. I called Enoch later on the same day of our shared verbal assault to announce my triumph over the seemingly immovable, monolithic mass of junk in the garage. He didn't believe me, and the items I wanted removed never were hauled away. As far as I know they remain in their same locations to this day a quarter century later. I felt a great sense of accomplishment anyway, because I had completed the impossible and won our argument within hours.

When the garbage truck finally arrived the two men assigned to the task stared at the wall of waste in disbelief, and begrudgingly began the task of hauling everything away. We filled the garbage truck. They returned with another, and we filled that one too! This was certainly talked about for some time, and is an enduring argument against the taxpayer subsidization of waste hauling. There was no limit to the amount of material we could throw away. Zero incentive existed to reduce our waste stream.

10

MY CRAZY DAD

Enoch persists in the snide comment that he's the closest thing to a dad that I ever had, but he never sucked on my toes to prevent frostbite damage in extreme cold, or on the same frigid day, put those frozen feet against his bare chest.

He also never did crazy things like take a 7-year-old on an odyssey that stretched along the Michigan lakefront for seven miles and several hours, leading all the way to the closed Racine Zoo well after dark. On that particular journey Dad and I mainly walked the sandy beach, but occasionally had to climb significant obstacles or shimmy along cliffs over deep water. We planned on turning around hours before, but were having too much fun to do so. Reaching the zoo, we walked up from the beach to dimly lit streets in search of a bus stop. Finding a self-service vegetable stand, we bought the largest tomato I had ever seen for ten cents. This left him just enough money for bus fare, and I chowed down on the entire thing for a late supper as we rode back to his apartment in exhaustion. I remember the experience vividly. It likely had a hand in shaping my lifelong love of hiking and the outdoors.

Camping trips with Dad also involved ambitious feats of physical exertion that I was proud of. Mere days after I learned to ride a bike without the use of training wheels, we biked around the full eight-mile perimeter of Mackinac Island in the state of Michigan. I was exhausted as we completed the loop, and coasted down a steep hill into the bustling town filled with tourists where we had begun hours earlier. As my bike picked up speed I lost control while Dad hollered from behind, "HIT THE BRAKES!" While screaming in terror, I careened down the hill as if I was saddled astride a rocket breaking the sound barrier. I barely managed to remain upright on the bicycle that must have approached a speed of 25 miles per hour. My trajectory carried me straight into a large horse's ass, off which my head violently ricocheted. I missed the hole, in the center of the plump target, by a mere inch. The horse, hitched up to a post, never saw me coming. Amazingly, it did not kick me. Given the position of my head after the crash, this could have been fatal.

Dad and I crawled under electric fences and followed the edges of farms and fields in order to reach fishing holes. On one such trip I was shocked three times by the fence. Charged up for a large cow, the electrocution daisy-chained through every cell of my body simultaneously at the speed of light. Repeated jolts brought a level of exhaustion somewhat akin to being struck by lightning. Perhaps that was the plan!

The day he moved out of the house he bought with Mom

was uneventful. I was only four years old, and didn't fully grasp the gravity of the situation. The night prior to this permanent tear in our family I had set an entire wall of the kitchen on fire by placing a soggy English muffin into the toaster, which promptly shorted out from all the moisture. Mom was working. Dad was jobless, again. Flames violently licked up to the ceiling while Dad was busy sawing logs on the living room couch as soundly as Rip Van Winkle. I yelled and shook him violently while he continued to snore impassively. By this time the growing blaze lit up the living room in a bright orange reflection from the kitchen. Mom returned home just in time to save us from destruction. Perhaps she snapped her fingers to make the fire go away? I'm not certain. It was a serious conflagration measuring eight to ten feet wide, while also darkening the ceiling. It was the last straw for her. Divorce papers were filed the next day. The blackened wall was concealed behind cheap wallpaper.

Dad moved into a cockroach-infested apartment in Milwaukee that I hated. From there he moved into a room within an impressive mansion with a number of other quirky roommates. The scene was reminiscent of a sitcom with all the crazy characters there. I recall Dick Springer, his ever-present robe, and a serious case of halitosis. Dad shared a bathroom with Reese, a 20-something who looked like a rock star with a large plume of permed hair, who took a shining to introducing me to his record collection. He played his rock music very loud. The son of the owner, Sam, must have been in his 50s. He still lived at home, had a speech impediment that made him nearly unintelligible, and had a mild case of mental retardation. He always seemed to be pointing and yelling at me or Dad's dog, Pandy, who lived outside.

Christmas was magical in the mansion, and yet incongruous in many respects. The large living area, boasting a wide staircase leading up to the residents' rooms, was host to a massive 20-foot-tall Christmas tree. The balcony outside the door to my dad's room overlooked the impressive scene. From here an adult could lean over, reaching high up, to place the star at the top of the tree.

Typically I celebrated Christmas with Dad several days after the holiday, and yet my gifts made for an embarrassingly large pile under the tree all by themselves. He adored showering me with gifts at this time of year. This left me uneasy. I knew he was poor, and unable to keep up with weekly $50 child support payments. Mom was always sure to remind me of this. He finally completed paying off these payments about when I reached the age of 21 (three years behind schedule). I visited him every other weekend, and generally we had a great time.

When I was six he built an impressive ant farm unlike anything money can buy. It was approximately 18 inches tall and 18 inches wide, with sandy loam soil sandwiched between two pieces of glass. To fill it we searched a field near Grandma's house until we found a large anthill that stood nearly three feet high. Inside were thousands of large and feisty ants that refused to have their colony destroyed without putting up a fight. Bites from the red and black ants were quite painful. The light sandy soil was extremely easy to excavate, however, and our work was quick. Within the crater I scooped perhaps three dozen worker ants into a Hills Brothers coffee can while Dad worked hard and fast to extend the large crater toward the center of the earth. On and on he dug in search of the queen, pausing for only brief moments to brush off the hundreds of ants that crawled up his pant legs that were tucked into his now soiled socks. By the time Dad was standing waste-deep in the large hole he was drenched in sweat and contemplating whether or not to give up on finding royalty. Incidentally, queen ants have been known to live for up to 30 years! We hoped to create a self-sustaining colony.

Finally he found the queen down near what we figured must have been the bottom. She was huge in size, and easy to identify. After he scooped her into the coffee can I asked if it was warmer way down deep in the ground from all the magma in the earth's core. He put his hand to the soil saying, "Just a bit."

It was a trick transferring the angry insects to the narrow ant farm, but after we succeeded in doing so they quickly went to work. Eventually their entire new universe was filled to capacity with various tunnels and caverns used for different purposes, such as food storage, egg and larvae care, etc. He lived with this in his single room in the mansion off Highway 38 for an entire summer. Ultimately, following a few evenings of unseen creatures biting him and causing itching, he gave the ants their freedom. Perhaps an unknown mite was living with them, and found a feast by boring into my dad's flesh. The itching stopped after the ants left the scene.

He did things like throw me a birthday party with 12 kids I didn't know, or wake me up at 4:00 in the morning to view a bright orange full moon as he stood outside in his underwear. I picked up an appreciation for everyday beauty from him.

He also took it upon himself to be incredibly irrational, such as pulling me out of kindergarten for an entire afternoon just so we could enjoy strawberry shortcake on top of a hill with a view that involved a steep climb. On a later date he pulled me out of the same school and drove me five hours north to Grandma and Grandpa's house without Mom's permission or foreknowledge. She ended up tilting into full panic mode, which ultimately shifted to rage when I was finally returned the next day. In 1980, before Amber Alerts existed, the sheriff simply knocked on Grandma's door and told my dad he'd need to return me home by the following morning.

By the time I reached the age of ten, he had moved in and out of a number of low-level laborer jobs and was now mowing lawns for a landscaping company. He lived in a nondescript apartment building on Romayne Avenue in Racine, Wisconsin. There was a marvelous empty field across the street that we took full advantage of. Over the course of nearly an entire Saturday we built an incredible grass hut by bundling the waist-high vegetation into segments that were fitted together. I still cannot figure out how he managed to fasten it together into such a sturdy structure. It looked like something one would find out on the savannah in Africa, and remained standing a month later. We sat in there and watched birds through gaps in the wall.

While he did other cool things, such as sprinkle Pixie Dust on my head from a jar filled with glowing fireflies before bed so I could fly in my dreams and house an antique train set that impressively consumed two 4 X 8 sheets of plywood and were connected by two bridges we constructed, Dad has always found a way to persistently irritate and humiliate me. I never once invited him to school functions. No matter how much I coached him ahead of time, he did things like stand up in the middle of the audience and conduct the orchestra with his boisterous outstretched arms. This produced chuckles and questions from the other kids, "Who's dad is that??!!!!" After the last song of the concert he unleashed the loudest high-pitch shrill of a whistle you've ever heard, and yelled out, "Bravo! BRAVO!" Upon leaving the crowded hallway with my mom I did my best to sneak out without his noticing us. I'm not proud of this.

While playing tennis with him near his home in Milwaukee on a stiflingly hot day I removed my shirt once. Lets just say I never did something this reckless again, unless we were swimming. Our court, of four available, was the only one in use. Additionally, I carefully scanned the horizon in every conceivable direction to verify that nobody was coming. As a self-conscious thirteen or fourteen-year-old boy, my bright, white, skinny chest, with two skinny Mr. Potato Head arms dangling from each side, was something I ardently kept concealed. It seemed safe to expose myself just this once, because the heat and humidity were oppressive. Within minutes the most beautiful, well-developed, high school girls that I had ever seen suddenly appeared without warning. I was horrified to have exposed my blinding whiteness to the angelic creatures, so I nonchalantly raced to the sideline to stretch my t-shirt over the bulging biceps that graced my 95-pound frame. I returned to the baseline to serve a ball to my Dad. From a distance of 80 feet—with the most beautiful girls on earth positioned a mere 40 feet away—he cluelessly hollered over, "WHY DID YOU PUT YOUR SHIRT BACK ON?" Not wanting to arouse interest in the conversation, I attempted to wordlessly waive off the question. This only piqued his interest.

"WHY DID YOU PUT YOUR SHIRT BACK ON?"

"Never mind Dad. I was cold I guess."

"WAS IT BECAUSE OF THE GIRLS?"

That was the last straw. Enraged and humiliated, I walked back to his house without looking back or uttering a single word as Dad unabashedly yelled for me to come back and finish the game. He had no concept of how embarrassing such scenes are to a young teenage boy. Today I find the story so amusing that I'm almost glad it happened, and yet I continue to wrestle with these same feelings any time I'm in public with him to this day.

Dad attended a Pentecostal church one mile away from my house. It was CRAZY pandemonium every week! The famous scene from *The Blues Brothers* movie only briefly touches the level of intensity the place reached during particularly wild Sundays or Wednesday nights. Dozens of "spirit-filled" worshippers raced down and across the aisles. One individual enjoyed spinning in a whirling dervish manner like a top with his arms outstretched. The sound of hundreds speaking in tongues—unintelligible holy gibberish that is purported to be in a heavenly tongue sounding like "Lalalalala shareem dullulululululululululu a MAHALA MASHACKALACKA"—filled the air. Sometimes a hush fell over the expansive sanctuary, capable of seating 2,000 souls, and a man would stand up and shout out a message in tongues. This made me unbelievably uncomfortable. Then the congregation remained expectantly silent for a minute, aside from the murmurs of praying in tongues that was nearly as constant as crooning cicadas, and someone would stand up and shout out the interpretation in English. This produced even greater unease when the interpreter inevitably started out with, "I AM THE LORD GOD. " This was followed by an exhortation, rebuke, an instruction, or all three.

Keep in mind that my portrayal of the experience of tongues is based upon an obscure sect that adheres to "Oneness Pentecostalism." Without burdening the reader with specifics, the many aberrant teachings have disfigured their faith into what reputable theologians contend is a cult. Many women have never cut their hair, keeping Rapunzel-like strands bound up in a bun for practicality's sake, always wear long dresses, and never wear makeup. Both sexes are burdened under the weight of rigid standards of "personal holiness," which only serve to obscure the point of their frenetic religiosity.

This was not your typical mass or worship service. It dragged on for three or four hours during powerful "moves of the spirit." Typically I slept or hid under the pew when I was between the ages of five and seven. On one occasion Dad walked up to the front to play his trombone in the band, and I heard some rich bastard say to his wife, "Have you seen anyone dressed like that before in your life?" Never say something like that about someone in public. I wish I had the confidence to have turned around with my unkempt hair and dirty clothes, and look him straight in the eyes while saying, "I heard you, you finely dressed hypocrite." I hated going there for years afterward.

During a friendless spell in ninth grade I biked the mile to
this church on Wednesdays, Sunday mornings, and
sometimes even on Sunday nights, as I searched for meaning
and purpose. I even got myself baptized without telling either
Mom or Dad. In this church, however, it was as if the
experience was meaningless because I wasn't filled with the
Holy Ghost, which they fallaciously believe is only evidenced
by speaking in tongues afterward. I was fired up about
church for a while, much to the chagrin of my mom, who
concluded arguments on the matter by hurling the insult of,
"You're just like your dad!" The fervency of my faith
dwindled, though, because I had zero friends in the faith.
With the benefit of hindsight I am thankful for not having
fallen down the rabbit hole into a not-so-wonderful land of
rigid religiosity that was disconnected from the real world.

In middle school and high school my visits with Dad
gradually dwindled down to one Saturday per month. This
made the annual weeklong camping trips with him essential
to maintaining a connection. At this stage it felt like we were
hillbillies, like the Clampetts, as we meandered through
campgrounds with a beat-up old car and an ancient canvas-
covered canoe pockmarked with unsightly patches. Our
canvas tent from the 1950s contributed to the feeling. Back in
the 1980s and early '90s these were far from cool among the
rest of the campers who were awash in all the newest and
latest equipment and vehicles to my insecure and watchful
eyes.

Every trip, without exception, was marked by a blowout that

cast all eyes in our direction from dozens of campsites as the record seemed to skip and everyone froze, not knowing how to react. It could be a sharp pinch of his hand while trying to get that last aluminum tent pole into a pocket, or more commonly a small burn of the finger while cooking a meal over the fire. In retrospect these instances are hilarious, but at the time were cause for deep shame and embarrassment. They always ran through the same verbiage in the same order:

"OH.. GAWD-AH! OH SHIT-AH! OHHHHH," leading to this full string of obscenities at the top of his lungs following a great breath-taking pause:

SHIT!!!

FUCK!!!

ASSHOLE!!!

SHIT!!!

FUCK!!!

ASSHOLE!!!

Sometimes Dad ran through the same litany a third time. Then, with his voice finally becoming hoarse, he ended with a final taking of the Lord's name in vain with great cadence in his voice, "OH>>>>> GAWD-AH!!!!!!!!!"

Ten minutes later he'd be right as rain. The intended

recipient of the outburst was nobody in particular, but rather the totality of the universe. The entire cosmos seemed to shake in response, with all of us having encountered an emotion-releasing tremor. Sometimes I was the cause of the pent-up rage due to my own anger issues. Dad says I have an angry-gene like my mom.

Due to his great aversion to pain, getting hurt, or being sick, I rarely let on when something was wrong. A hint of a mild cold resulted in unceasing cajoling to eat raw garlic and onions, which he took bites out of like apples. Inevitably such conversations could only end in one way, with me screaming at him in exasperation to just, "SHUT UP AND LEAVE ME ALONE!" Thus, when I drove the business end of a small axe a full quarter-inch into the meat of my shin at the tender age of 12, I remained silent. The entire length of the blade had sunk into my flesh. I was attempting to use it to cut some firewood on a cold predawn morning of late summer. We were staying in a rustic cabin on Mirror Lake in the Upper Peninsula of Michigan near Lake Superior in Porcupine Mountains Wilderness State Park, which required a four-mile hike from where Dad parked the car. It was our last day at the private cabin. Later that day, following a two-hour hike and a seven-hour drive, I'd be back home in my smelly house in what seemed like a distant universe.

Dad emerged from his bunk fifteen minutes later to inexplicably find me standing in the lake past my knees. It was 45°F and foggy, and there I was in blue, nylon shorts as if I was perfectly comfortable. Possessing no gauze pads, and afraid to ask if my dad had any, I remained in the cold water for a full twenty minutes as my legs went numb. My wound was a real gusher, and frightening. The blood kept pouring from me, clouding the water with redness similar to the effect of the bullhead being devoured by my piranhas a few chapters back. Eventually my patience won out. The bleeding finally stopped to my great relief. Though I was profoundly uncomfortable with chill—I had lost all feeling of my legs and wound—I remained in the water longer just to be sure. Then, with my dad skulking about with obvious concern, I was forced to wait for an opportune time to return to dry land without being seen. I successfully feigned indifference to the cold temperature and fog, pretending to be soaking weary legs while enjoying one last morning of peace. With his back turned, engaged in some camp chore, I seized the opportunity by racing to the cabin in my bare feet. Quickly, I changed into blue jeans, which I did not remove until I was safely at home. Though it was much too warm later that day to hike out of the wilderness while carrying a duffle bag and gear with both arms full—we didn't own fancy backpacks—while wearing long pants, I was careful to not betray the slightest hint of discomfort.

That evening, after peeling off the disgusting jeans, I washed my wound that was now grossly clotted with blood and thickly scabbed over. It was imperative to conceal the gash from Mom as well. She would have blamed my dad. I also feared that she could have put an end to our annual weeklong camping trips. I lived for these escapes to wilderness during the long summer months that otherwise seemed to drag on with no end in sight. I successfully kept the accident a secret, and several others. Neither Mom nor Dad has ever been told this story until they read these words just now. I haven't provided them with advance copies of this book either. They are following along in these stories from the viewpoint of a lost little boy just like you.

Even though the yearly trips to Mackinac Island, the Porcupine Mountains, and numerous other locales, were permeated with arguments, anger, and frustration, the return home was always surreal. At the end of the long drive home, he turned into the subdivision and savored the last two miles through the neighborhood. The entire rest of the drive he exceeded the speed limit as if in a race, even as I protested in fear that a cop would pull him over. As soon as he pulled into that last stretch he became visibly depressed and reflective. He realized we wouldn't be seeing each other for a while, and slowed his old beater down as if we were bringing up the rear of a parade. The big baby blue 1976 Chevy Nova, pock-marked with rust, floated along at a pace slower than tractor speed, as if for Ms. Daisy. I slunk down low to avoid being seen. My extreme apprehension and anxiety must have been a great deal like one of the many space dogs that returned to earth in Soviet space capsules as they slowly floated down to the ocean after the parachute opened following re-entry. Of course I was embarrassed, but I was most troubled about the return to reality.

The journey home culminated in one of two ways. Following one such trip my mom was lying listlessly despondent on the couch, chain-smoking. The entire house was filled with an eye-burning haze of cigarette smoke with all the windows sealed shut, even though Mom wasn't a smoker to my knowledge. She had ingested so much nicotine that she cast the appearance of someone strung out on heroine. Thus, one of Mom's responses was that of a deep depression marked by a lack of purpose or energy that took her days from which to emerge. The far more common greeting following hours of driving, however, was an eruption of volcanic rage.

Mom stormed out of the house like an angry hornet, oftentimes accompanied by Enoch, hollering obscenities in the front yard at full tilt within the earshot of many neighbors. On one occasion, after the screaming subsided and the door closed, an unfamiliar sound of nearby glass breaking suddenly alarmed Mom and me. Then, as if in slow motion like the viewing of a distant asteroid entering the atmosphere, we observed a rock coming through the front window. My dad was strafing the house with rocks due to his own resentment and anguish. Mom's massive temper met the challenge by erupting in its full force and fury. She exited the house and struck my dad in the face while still in mid-stride without an ounce of hesitation. His eyeglasses shattered on the ground an instant later, bringing everyone back to earth. Both were sorry for what they had done, but such incidents are far too much weight for a young child to bear who loves both his parents. That night I cried myself to sleep with what seemed to be an unending wellspring of tears.

Today Dad lives in the house his mother and father purchased in 1943 in northern Wisconsin. Here he endeavors to irrefutably prove the truth of the old saying in demonstrating that, "There's a sucker born every minute." While he ekes out a living by working up to 30 hours per week wrapping meat in the local grocery store for the paltry sum of $7 an hour—remaining well within Social Security's personal income limits in his retirement by the way—his real job is to serve as the number one mark for every huckster in the nation. His desk is crowded with junk mail, which he insists on scrupulously examining. Stacks of boxes contain offers delivered daily to his mailbox promising future wealth or youthful health into perpetuity. Years ago one of these ads introduced him to the wonderful world of blue-green algae. Offering an open foil pack to me, he bursts out, "I take 30 of these a day. They give me lots of energy!"

If anybody doesn't need extra energy, it's him. One of his problems is too much unchanneled energy, in fact. Sometimes you can see it buzzing, electrically, through his entire fidgeting body and unfocused eyes that can take on a glazed-over difficult-to-describe wildness. Once, for example, while my aunt and uncle sat visiting in his living room, he laid down on the floor and start spinning on his side as if he was running in place. The same familiar embarrassment swept over me, though I was well into my 30's.

The massive quantity of mail he receives each day, which approaches the level dramatized in A Miracle on 34th Street when numerous duffel bags of letters from the children of the world are delivered to Santa Claus in the courtroom, serves to simultaneously prop up the United States Postal Service with much needed cash and necessitate the felling of trees the world over to meet the demand. Following one recent vacation that pulled him away from home for six delivery days, he showed up at the local post office to retrieve his held mail. The clerk behind the counter was incredulous when he handed her a large banana-box sized tote, asking,

"You want me to use this huge box for a week's worth of mail?"

"Yes, please."

"Ok." (Insert eye roll here.)

She returned five minutes later with the box filled to overflowing saying, "You really did need this box!"

The seriousness with which he pursues his true vocation does not merely consist in reviewing and responding to offers by mail. He also relishes being had by unscrupulous used car salesmen that confidently exude success. The same goes for encounters with financially well-off people that attempt to evangelize him into various cults. More than once I have had to talk him down from one of these ledges. Additionally, he entertains each and every telemarketer that reaches him by phone.

In the year 2013, two decades after the birth of the World Wide Web, Dad contacted me to excitedly tell of a new business opportunity he had just invested in by making a credit card payment over the phone in the amount of four or five thousand dollars. Keep in mind that the man has lived in poverty all his life. This is a very large sum for him—several multiples of his available savings, actually. He asked me, "Did you know that people are going to be buying much more of their goods over the Internet in the future?" Thus, even though he had barely any knowledge of the Internet and no connection to it at home, he had hopes of creating his own web-based business. I freaked out. This is my most common response.

Since the angry-gene I inherited apparently permeates every

fiber of my being, the majority of our conversations involve me lecturing him about the need to save money and STOP entertaining offers by phone and mail. He has virtually no savings. One of my deepest fears is that he'll lose his home and that I'll be left holding the bag. It could happen at any time. I bemoan the fact that I am the parent in our relationship.

My dad, like my mom, drives me nuts. Absolutely crazy actually. Visits to this day continue to be marked by a constant furrow on my face, and yet I've never doubted his love for me. For this reason I never once wished for another father.

11

I ONLY HAVE EYEBROWS FOR YOU

The nadir of my existence came suddenly and decisively in September of 1990. Having a crush on a girl, I sat alone in our empty (yet very full) house after the second day of my freshman year at J.I. Case High School in Racine, Wisconsin. Peering into the mirror for guidance—never a good idea—I decided to gussy myself up a bit. I found a large pair of sharp steel scissors, and began trimming my eyebrows.

A snip here, a snip there, and pretty soon the entire sink was lined with small hairs, as if a young Santa Claus had mowed down his beard prior to a big date in an effort to transform himself into a well-groomed young man. I had been felling trees without paying attention to the forest. By the time I paused to survey the lay of the land, I was aghast to discover several holes that looked like swaths of clearcut in what remained of the jungle. In a panic I thinned the thicker portions to even things out, and was left with dainty patches of blond peach fuzz over each eye. Since I have dark brown hair it was as if they had vanished. It looked like my forehead, already uncomfortably large, had endured a rare form of chemotherapy. As the cutting of Samson's locks diminished his strength, so the washing down the drain of my individual eyebrow hairs swept away any good looks or hope I had in winning the girl's heart.

I returned to school the following morning, the third day in a far-away high school with few acquaintances, to quickly discover that my careful work with the eyebrow pencil hadn't fooled anyone. Hours had been spent carefully coloring in dark brown eyebrows. Any loss of concentration or impatience resulted in a discernible line rather than the desirable subtle variations in shading. Within five minutes of arriving at school an older kid was up close in my face, announcing his discovery to the world.

This was a traumatic end-of-the-world upheaval that called for moving to another planet. To be new in a school of 2,000 students, grinding through such circumstances, was to be an outcast bobbing and floating in a sea of despair. Life was a wasteland bereft of joy. Hopes and dreams dried up like rivulets in the heat of the desert.

I tried my usual class clowning, but nothing worked. They laughed at me, not with me. This was the most noteworthy event in the entire school that year. Everyone knew who I was. I garnered the notoriety I craved, except it was the wrong kind. All 2,000 souls, and this bears repeating because this could be the population of a decent-sized town, knew who I was. They all pointed and laughed, including mentally impaired children in wheelchairs. Good students, bad students, jocks, preps, gang-bangers, nerds, burn-outs, everyone in band, metal heads, wimps, teachers (yes, teachers), janitors, hall monitors, lunch ladies, fat kids, and absolutely every other conceivable group of humanity elbowed their friends to point me out as if I was a celebrity while I tried to keep my head down to go unnoticed through the packed hallways.

This was a disaster of epic proportions. I was lowest of the low. Impressing the girl with good looks and charm was out of the question, and the least of my concerns. My friend Steve jettisoned me like useless space garbage. I had no friends. Figuring out where to sit in the lunchroom was like being an earthworm attempting to burrow into quantum physics. This trial set a tone that endured all four years. It irreparably damaged the entire high school experience. I considered suicide as an option, if for no other reason than to make my tormentors feel bad.

My habit of skipping school switched into high gear. I missed 45 or more days of school each year until I graduated with honors four years later. It was shockingly simple to get away with this nefariousness. I simply called my mother, already at work, and asked her to call school to advise I was sick whenever I "missed" the bus. Mom didn't like being complicit in this scam, but she was virtually powerless to do anything about it while at work. Plus, I was an excellent salesman by pointing to my stellar grades as proof that everything was going fine. I remained upbeat and positive, while reassuring her that my grades wouldn't slip. My problems had to do with a hollowing out of my very foundation. I kept this a secret even as the world was caving in around me.

I wish I could point to adventurous activities on these days
off. Instead I spent hours alone in front of the television for
lack of knowledge of anything else to do. School was too
much to bear. I felt profoundly unloved as an alien in the
company of others who seemed to merely tolerate me. I
remained cloistered within our house of junk, sealed off from
the world in a putrid ecosystem, scavenging for ancient
freezer-burned TV dinners. Searching for meaning in life, I
watched the Catholic channel, EWTN, religiously. Mother
Angelica, the elderly nun who founded the cable channel,
was one of my favorites. She was a wizened and loving
grandmotherly figure who seemed to gently communicate the
"answers." If there had been a Catholic church near my
house I would have signed up in a flash.

While it wasn't a nun that ultimately flew in to the rescue,
hope was on the way.

12

ANDY

A ray of sunshine emerged from an unlikely place in the spring of my freshman year. A fellow trumpet player, sitting one chair ahead of me in the hierarchy, invited me on a camping trip with his family. I was never invited to anything, let alone something as unbelievable as this. Even today my eyes well up with tears when I reflect on the impact Andy Walczynski and his family had on me. I was warmly enfolded into his family, offered a seat at their table, and was given a brother.

This family was the greatest gift of my childhood, and the absolute intervention of the Almighty. Dickensian images of paupers being raised from rags to riches spring to mind. It is not possible to overstate their influence on a life that otherwise may have ended prematurely. Friendship with Andy salvaged the next two years of my life, and enabled the very meat of the high school experience to become palatable. I am so overcome with gratitude that I can hardly move to the next paragraph. It is as if these memories plug a hole in my heart that needs to be accessed with surgical precision.

We left together on a sunny spring afternoon after school in May of 1991 for my first camping trip with a family. Mom dropped me off at his house, and Andy's parents welcomed me with open arms. I wasn't accustomed to being warmly invited into a nice home. Mentally, I was programmed to wait outside like hired help. I encountered an entirely different world as I sheepishly crossed the threshold. The rooms were spotlessly clean and designed for hospitality. This was a real home where relationships were cherished and children were nurtured to adulthood. Pictures graced the walls testifying to numerous life stages and a multitude of satisfying experiences they had shared.

After the minivan and pop-up camper were situated, we headed west toward the setting sun and a horizon full of new possibilities. I felt like the luckiest kid on earth as I was plucked from among the great herd of unwashed rabble.

The most unforgettable part of the trip involved sitting in one of the captain's chairs in the rear of the van. A loving mother and father adorned the front as they enjoyed an easy, casual conversation devoid of swearing or acrimony. I was accustomed to traveling with Mom in the front seat of her Dodge Omni. When I did ride in the rear it was like being crammed into a stress-filled projectile hurtling through space as she and Enoch screamed at each other or me.

Sitting in the back of Andy's van, among such peace, was simply amazing. I could have dwelled there silently for hours, basking in warmth like a reptile takes in the sun. The experience was overwhelming, and took me off guard. A dad driving the car with the loving mother next to him was a unique and precious site to behold. I allowed the peaceful atmosphere to seep into my very bones. I drank it in, and savored it. This was my "balm in Gilead." A feeling of safety, like that of a baby bird high up in a nest with its mother, washed over me. I thought of Andy, sitting alongside and oblivious to these new positive feelings within me, as a kind of brother while pretending this was my very own stable family.

After an hour that seemed to end too soon, we pulled into a crowded, virtually tree-less RV park. Most of the "campers" had large rigs boasting full bathrooms, living rooms, kitchens, and televisions, so we were thought of as roughing it. The "park" had a mini-golf course, arcade, basketball court, and numerous entertainment options for a world seemingly incapable of entertaining itself. Even then I would have preferred a more wilderness-like setting. Nevertheless, it was an awesome vacation. We had fun from sunup to sundown as we partook in all the offerings. We quickly became best friends. This joy-filled weekend was like a life-saving blood transfusion. It came at a time when I needed a friend the most. Enjoying all aspects of family life for two full uninterrupted days was as incredible to me as being on safari.

I sat in silent introspection during the journey home. I was grieved to transition from stable family to my broken, empty home and persistently lonely world. More pressing, however, was figuring out how to handle the inescapable reality that they were driving directly to my house. The prospect terrified me. I tumbled through the possibilities with increasing desperation as each mile passed. I was certain that Andy would help me with my bags, and I couldn't think of a way to keep him out of my messy house. As far as I knew, it was filthier and more packed with junk than any other in the world. I still haven't been into its equal after nearly four decades of life on this planet. Unable to find a way out of this conundrum, I decided to play it cool. I resolutely determined not to betray any emotion or anxiety, or they would sense that something was wrong. Therefore I eased back into the conversation, acting as if I was simply enjoying the ride.

My heart pounded as we pulled up the driveway of my little hovel, and yet I still maintained a calm demeanor. An unexpected flash of genius came to the rescue when I discovered Mom wasn't home. I am still rather proud of how I adeptly handled this crisis, and am tempted to put the following on my resume. I pretended to not have the key to the house, and asked them to wait in the van as I climbed in through the back window. Having done so, I walked through the home and emerged from the unlocked front door looking relieved at having gained access. My theatrics provided the perfect distraction.

I confidently walked to the van with a triumphant smile. "Thanks for waiting to make sure I got in all right." Then I grabbed my bags and walked alone to the house. The quizzical look on his dad's face betrayed the fact that he could tell something was wrong. My performance was the finest I could muster, however. I was rather skillful at nonchalantly keeping people out of this house that was my main source of shame.

The stench of dog (and unfortunately my own) urine, feces, rotting food, mold, and only God knows what else, immediately hit me upon entering the house. Opening the front door was like breaking the seal from a can of sardines. The saturated atmosphere within rushed to consume the fresh air outside. Quick shut the door before the whole world is contaminated! When Andy and his family drove off, crushing loneliness immediately overwhelmed me. My playful dog Curly eagerly licked my face as I wept by myself among all our junk that barely offered any place to sit. This was a can't-catch-your-breath style of weeping, and one that required a full rehydrating glass of water along with a face washing afterward. It was a complete derailment.

Within minutes some semblance of equilibrium returned, and I adjusted to the point of not noticing my surroundings. The television was my coping mechanism, escape, and therapist. The idiot box was turned on almost immediately upon any arrival, and remained on until going to sleep. We never enjoyed a quiet day or evening at home without it. To be without the TV was to be faced with the reality of our situation. Making our home more livable was impossible. The enormity of the problem was beyond us. Andy never did catch a glimpse of our mounds of junk or of my animal friends, but provided the perfect escape from it.

Each summer day, like a fly drawn to honey, I biked 20 miles each way to hang out with Andy at his house. Frequently we'd begin a long bike ride of up to 100 miles from there! We enjoyed century rides from time to time to random spots on the map, such as the town of Wilmot, Wisconsin, or long boring rides into Illinois. Such adventures were incredibly satisfying and built confidence. After riding the 50 miles to the small town of Wilmot, for example, there was nothing to do but enjoy a Twinkie at a gas station and turn around for home where we may have rested a little before playing basketball or tennis. I was pulled over by a police officer for the first time on this particular journey, and thought that was pretty remarkable. Frequently after enjoying an amazing meal with his family where we had the opportunity to share the adventures of the day at the dinner table, I biked home in near exhaustion. Sometimes I finished long after the sun receded beyond the horizon in virtual darkness, after completing up to 140 miles in a day at the young age of 15.

Incredibly, I awoke the morning after ready to two-wheel it to his house all over again for a minimum of another 40 miles by bike. The next day found us riding to a well-apportioned fitness center exclusive to Johnson Wax employees, where his father worked, to play tennis at the best possible location. Even though this favorite spot to play was located roughly equidistant between our respective homes, I very often took the opportunity to ride back home with him so I could enjoy even just a small amount of time with Andy and his family. There was no reason to return home sooner. Usually Mom was at work, and for me the place was a barren, vacuous, hollowed out wasteland that exposed my broken heart.

To Andy's credit, he repeatedly offered to journey to my house in an effort to take turns with expending the energy that a 40-mile round-trip required. I quickly eschewed the idea, and went through great pains to avoid complaining about the trip. Day after day, usually five a week, I was in or around his house for much of the day. The patience of his parents to endure this is a marvelous wonder to me. Additionally, I was invited on occasional weekend camping trips to Wisconsin Dells with the family as well. Surely they must have tired of seeing me around! On rare days of heavy rain I stayed home, and occasionally Andy had other plans. These were days of listless depression that involved a monotonous diet of daytime television and microwaved food.

The Walczynski family remains a near-perfect example of an entire family having a positive impact on the life of a child. I don't believe they were conscious of the fact that they were reaching out to me in a powerful way by simply opening up their lives to me. The beauty of the situation is that they didn't have the faintest idea they were rescuing me. This was the love of Jesus just overflowing naturally. I recall very few wise words of advice being spoken into my life. They were just present, and an example of a healthy family. I joined them at Mass once or twice, and was completely baffled by all the kneeling, signs of the cross, and rigid formality. Prior to this my only exposure to faith was the Pentecostal church referenced earlier, and I greatly enjoyed the contrast. The liturgy and seemingly choreographed movements within the Catholic Church seemed remarkably holy and awe-inspiring. I commend this account to church groups, families, and any individual looking to be a pillar in the life of their community. Simply open your heart and life to others. Enfold them into your life, and you cannot help but be a blessing to them. Do not overthink it. You very well could be saving a life without even realizing it.

Andy's father ultimately received a promotion, and his family moved to sunny southern California after our junior year in high school. This left me bereft of friends or any positive family in my life. I privately cried my eyes out.

13

EVERYTHING IS MEANINGLESS

After my high school cross country team failed to win the state title in my third and final attempt, I went on a mindless run in freezing rain the very next day to punish myself. Hearing a train coming, I decided to race it to the crossing. Running on the gravel shoulder, because the road was now quite icy, I was in an all-out sprint to the tracks. At the last minute I looked to my left to gauge the progress of the speeding locomotive. To my surprise the train was nearly there. Feeling fully committed to the race as if it was a game, although in this case a tie wouldn't go to the runner, I kicked into high gear. About a second later I leaped across the tracks like a super hero.

I could see the train's engineer screaming "NO!" while waving me away frantically. I was so close to being smashed like a bug that I literally had to jump sideways across the tracks in order to streamline my shape as I passed before it. If I hadn't turned in mid-air to the point where I was briefly facing the oncoming behemoth as I flew across the tracks, I would have become track kill. It was that close. Landing hard on the other side, facing the train (thus completing a 180 degree turn in mid-air), I immediately felt the wind of the train as it steamed past me at full velocity. I leaned my torso back to keep from being hooked by the train that was flying by mere inches away. The good Lord was looking out for me that day even though I had failed to look after myself.

Flush with adrenaline, and reveling in a feeling of enhanced aliveness, I raced the two miles home in some fear of being picked up by a squad car. Returning home, I removed wet running shoes and carefully stepped through my house as if avoiding land mines, while also stepping around obstacles of various shapes and sizes. The limited amount of open floor space, owing to the clutter in piles that ranged in height from an inch to seven or more feet (in a sense there was just one enormous pile because it was all conjoined in one contiguous blob), increased the odds that I would step directly into a wet puddle while in my bare feet. At all times there were numerous markings around the house from my beloved dog, Curly, and these came in the form of both numbers one and two. Generally you could find the piles of excrement, unless a shadow obscured it, thus causing the collision of the solid with the not-so-solid in the dreaded squish. On this particularly overcast day I made direct contact with squish. After clearing space for me to sit along the bathtub with my foot draped inside under the running faucet, I wept with a broken heart while considering the futility of my situation and the meaninglessness of it all.

After Andy left I seemed to lose the tether that held me to the ground. I had trouble seeing beyond immediate problems toward a greater purpose or any overarching meaning to my story. I had no close friends. There was zero direction in life and no guideposts. I was completely inept with girls, and this was of paramount concern. Watching my senior prom at home on television with Mom, I felt like a complete loser.

In the evenings I was routinely in violation of child labor laws by working until 10 pm or later as a busboy in a restaurant. The old Italian man that ruled the roost from a stool in the kitchen was reputedly in the mob, so I would never come out and say that I may have urinated on his seat cushion after punching out on my last day. In the evenings I returned home to uninspiring homework that robbed me of sleep. Frequently I fell asleep during classes.

I somehow maintained a GPA over 4.0. Many of the well-groomed kids in my classes were highly conscientious members of the National Honor Society (NHS). They all seemed to have a direction in which they were moving. I never fit in. Feeling like a misfit, I dropped out of NHS largely because one of the teachers that led it was annoyed by my habit of saying, "Hey," in the hallway instead of the more proper, "Hi." Several of these students came from wealthy families, were good looking, and were destined for significant scholarships in prestigious schools. I, on the other hand, felt like nothing. While I didn't have a death wish, I certainly didn't care whether I lived or died.

This manifested itself in reckless behavior, both because I really didn't care and also to prove that I wasn't a nerdy goodie-goodie. It was not a good idea for anyone to be walking across Nicholson Road at 7:10 am on a weekday. The straight-as-an-arrow road served as my racetrack to get to school. Frequently I had the needle buried in my Dodge Omni at 90 mph or better as I sought to stave off yet another detention due to tardiness. I'm fairly certain that I occasionally caught a little air on small hills.

Once, having missed homeroom, I raced through the halls to first period. The bell went off as I was entering an impossible slide from a full sprint in my Teva sandals while rounding the corner into the entryway. I slid directly into the door, dropping a morning's worth of books in an impressive splay across the floor. My head slammed into the tile for good measure. Everyone in geometry class laughed hysterically. I pretended everything was fine with my usual upbeat class clown demeanor, but was dying inside.

Behind my high school was a site used by cement trucks that had several trails crisscrossing the adjoining woods. Sometimes on muddy days when we didn't feel like engaging in a long hard run we snuck past the no trespassing sign and enjoyed getting dirty. The last time we did this I ran across what looked like a grey muddy pit. There was no sign marking danger, and it was not roped off. I fell into the sludge, which was apparently a very deep hole that was used to empty the watery excess from cement mixers after they were cleaned out. Soon I was up to my armpits and sinking fast. My teammates, with their muddy hands, struggled to get a firm grip on my outstretched arms. Five or six guys were working on getting me out of there as I nearly sank to my chin. My head went blank as I dangled limply in limbo between life and death. Unfortunately I really didn't care which way the story ended. Eventually I was safely extricated from the quicksand. Aside from mighty sore arms from all the tugging, I was uninjured.

Another favorite pastime was entering a car dealership with my trustworthy face, while feigning interest in buying a car so I could abuse it on the test drive. Once I had the sporty version of a 1992 Ford Tempo up to 120 mph on Highway 20 heading out of town with a couple "friends" laughing hysterically in the back seat. It was just another example of me trying to prove that I was a fun guy, but such stunts never won me the companionship that I craved. During my junior or senior year I acquired a Jeep Cherokee and delighted in taking others four-wheeling through impossible terrain during lunch hour. More than once we were marooned when it became stuck or broken down, which was really half the fun. Routinely we returned to school with the dark black vehicle plastered in mud to the point that you couldn't distinguish the color of the paint, and found a spotless sports car to sidle along next to for entertainment purposes. This also failed to win lasting friends.

A strong sense of isolation enveloped me like a blanket. I had always found solace in the outdoors, but I wasn't comfortable enough in my own skin to risk the possibility of being seen enjoying the woods by myself. As a result, I would occasionally bike to the Root River and sit under the bridge that spans it on Nicholson Road. It forms the boundary between Milwaukee and Racine County. I sat under the bridge like a troll, and was pleased to be invisible down there as the dirty waters of that river swirled past. This speaks volumes to the rampant pack mentality that plagues teenagers in our culture.

Rivers that serve as boundaries have always been a pull for me. It is as if they metaphorically represent something much greater. Perhaps they symbolize larger boundaries that if courageously crossed will lead into a wondrous new world.

PART TWO: FOUND

14

THE END OF THE BEGINNING

Labor Day weekend of 1995 was monumental. Camping 20 feet from the Canadian border on the Pigeon River in complete solitude, I sprawled out in my sleeping bag under the stars with a pile of books and a roaring campfire to provide warmth and light for reading. The curvature of the earth fit snugly into the small of my back. Feeling whole, content, and at peace for the first time, I reveled in the simplicity and clarity of a new life apart from the expectations of others.

At the university 150 miles to the south, thousands of students were packed into dorms and apartments in anticipation of a new school year. I was feeling free and elated to not be among them. My freshman year had been a disaster. Lacking any direction or ambition, I had immediately gone to college after high school solely because this was the conventional path. Though I graduated high school near the top of my class, I was drawn to the University of Minnesota-Duluth out of a ridiculous desire to have more opportunities to bounce around in my Jeep off-road in the great North Woods (which endured only three months of harsh treatment before breaking down). I hadn't even considered applying to any elite schools. In an effort to win the affection of others, I had gone through great pains throughout my life to prove to my peers that I was loads of fun and no smarter than anybody else.

And yet, I left home for college without a single friend. The adult world was a wide-open frontier to be navigated through trial and error without the benefit of guidance or mentors. Heavily recruited by the university's cross country running coach, which I later learned was due solely to the potential for my stellar grades to bump up the team's average, I quickly crapped the bed. I was completely unmotivated by my classes. Unable to make sense of the world, I had no further need of head knowledge. Attempts at a raucous life of partying fell equally flat. The wilderness was the only thing that made sense—bounding in beauty, order, and life—but hiking and paddling excursions into and along pristine lakes and forest only provided a temporary palliative relief to my condition.

Unexpectedly and thoroughly unplanned, immediately following the end of the spring term I found myself on a voyage of self-discovery that was more fruitful than I could have possibly imagined. Everything changed. All that was required of me was ample time and a teachable spirit, which I cheerfully provided. Untethered and liberated to pursue true north, all previous priorities and commitments had passed out of view below the southerly horizon. Deep wilderness, books, and experiences were a far more effective classroom. My first trimester was completed during the summer break. I was in the process of being reborn while undergoing a nine-month gestation in the womb of a newly emancipated life free of school, hoarding, and insecurities. I had removed myself from the bewildering maze of life's rat race that previously held me fast in a quagmire of meaninglessness. I could sense that I was still being molded and formed when summer ended much too quickly—not yet prepared to return to the same treadmill that led nowhere. A full sabbatical was needed, so I delayed my return to college. This was the best decision I ever made.

As presumptuous as this may sound, I had recently come to know the creator of all things. You know, God. It was inconceivable that the Lord of the universe was actually interested in me, but it was unmistakable. My conversion was complete and total. It began at the end of my freshman year of college when I awoke from a dream with such spiritual hunger that I turned to page one of the Bible, and devoured it for three days straight instead of going to classes. It culminated at a Christian retreat in Colorado with a prayer in which I surrendered my life, dreams, and hopes. My old self was entirely torn down, and a new life was being erected upon the ashes. The old heaviness and emptiness lifted, as if a great fog, and blew away.

Everything was new, different, and pregnant with meaning. My personality changed entirely. Fresh hobbies and interests sprang forth from the newly fertile soil of a renewed heart and mind. I was a new man delighting in learning about God and the world. It was as if I had been raised by wolves, and finally emerged from a lifetime of ignorance and deprivation. Everything that my fellow humans took for granted, I found to be utterly fascinating. Steeping myself in simple experiences, I gained greater understanding of the world and my interactions with it.

I was transfixed by all of creation. Sunsets mesmerized, newly discovered vistas enchanted, and I was captivated by newfound love and purpose. I began to hear the whisperings of God alongside a waterfall or babbling brook, in the wind whistling through the pines, or even while calm and alone in a quiet cabin.

I finally grasped the marriage of nature (beautiful and significant in and of itself) and the concept of creation (inextricably linked to the character of God) as being a way to learn more about the Creator through his handiwork. With virtually no distractions, I was coming to know him intimately as my father. A foundation was being laid for my entire future existence during this sabbatical. He became my source of peace, rest, comfort, joy, my reason for living. Scripture became enlivened for the first time as it rooted itself in my heart. I recorded the following Psalms in my journal after delighting in them as if basking in the hot sun of the first warm spring day:

> I am still confident of this:
> I will see the goodness of the Lord
> in the land of the living.
> Wait for the Lord:
> be strong and take heart
> and wait for the Lord.

Many are asking, "Who can show us any good?"
Let the light of your face shine upon us, O Lord.
You have filled my heart with greater joy
than when their grain and new wine abound.
I will lie down and sleep in peace,
for you alone, O Lord,
make me dwell in safety.

My thirst and zest to fully live life was insatiable and never abated as I maximized virtually every minute of each day. I was making up for 19 years of lost time, and was like a happy dog eagerly sucking marrow from a bone. On this new pilgrimage I hungered for knowledge and growth, and not just in the typical things most people deem to be spiritual. I found almost everything contained meaning spiritually, in that all things originated from the one source. Ultimately I found my way up the North Shore of Lake Superior in northern Minnesota where I worked at Cascade Lodge and Restaurant, endlessly tramped around the wilderness in my spare time, and took to reading like a fly to honey. I learned to experience joy and solitude, and joy in solitude, for the first time in my life.

15

WANDERLUST

Silence is a state of the soul. One is content to simply "be." All noise in the brain comes to a halt and you can finally listen. Being able to actually hear is incredibly satisfying. Creativity, love, peace, and awareness of your place in the universe, spring freely from this place. You are often at war with yourself to get there, but finally it arrives and envelops you like a persistent, yet gentle, snow blanketing the landscape.

By the time I got to the end of that summer—my first as an adult away from home—I had thrived while adventuring on a remarkable scale. I simply was not sitting still unless it was at the base of a waterfall or the crest of a vista many miles into the wilderness. If I wasn't working, I was exploring the Superior National Forest as earnestly and sincerely as if searching for the great Northwest Passage during the age of exploration. I grew in my faith and as a human being in leaps and bounds. Friendships bloomed in what previously had been a wasteland—now irrigated by a profound restlessness to experience, learn, and do more. It was as if I was learning to use all my available senses. Like Helen Keller, I ravenously craved more and more while learning to experience and interact with the world.

At night, well after dark, I read books for pleasure for the first time in my life. My mind was a clean slate that wanted to absorb anything I could get my hands on, much like that of a baby sucking on any and all objects for the sensory information. While devouring books as the rest of the world slept, mice actively went about their business in the ceiling above me in the tiny cabin dubbed the "Mouse House" where I lived. There must have been 100 or more rodents copulating in a wild orgy under that roof. At any time of day you could bang against the ceiling, and hear dozens of them scurrying off in all directions.

Daily, I hiked and hastily ran many miles through the beguiling forest to beat the setting sun or return to work on time. If I started work in the afternoon, the entire morning was spent ranging far afield up and down the shore of Lake Superior. Whenever I had any significant time off, usually just a day or so, I maximized it by striking out on ambitious expeditions. Whenever possible I used these trips to share my "discoveries" with new friends.

For example, on one such trip I had just 28 hours to pack in larger-than-life goals. I arranged for my good friend Dan to arrive from southern Minnesota to join me the minute I punched out of work at 3:30 p.m. in answering the alluring siren call of the North. I also delighted in introducing two

Irish exchange students, Mags and Kieren, to the Northwoods as we drove a total of 500 miles in exploring beautiful Ontario, Canada. I played the role of proud tour guide showing off my new back yard. These kids from Ireland typically hung out in their hotel room with the 20 or so other foreign workers in Grand Marais, Minnesota. Drinking seemed to be their favorite pastime. It was thrilling to provide them with their first authentic introduction to our forests and wildlife.

We swam in a river below Kakabeka Falls, the Niagara of the North, as a haze drifted overhead from some 415 separate forest fires that were then burning in northwest Ontario during the dry summer. We split a cheap room at Bob's Motel where we ventured across the parking lot to the Golden Nugget Bar. This was my first trip to a bar, legal age in Canada being 19, and the wildlife there was frightening. A horribly loud country band blared away, and women the age of my mom were dressed for a purpose as they danced the night away. In the rain we visited Ouimet Canyon, mined for amethysts, and finally capped it off with a trip through Sleeping Giant Provincial Park. This is a gorgeous park on an immense peninsula that boldly juts out into the ocean-like body of water and casts the appearance of a giant sleeping, with hills rising over 1200 feet from Lake Superior. Here we encountered a remarkably friendly black bear cub.

The bear was on the side of the road, so I stopped to allow for gawking as if we were on safari. The animal ambled right up to the car. Kieren, who had never even seen a bear before, had his window open. The look of wondrous terror on his face was precious as he could only frantically watch the window close painfully slowly whilst the cub poked its head into the top of the opening. A reckless individual certainly could have exited the vehicle to pet the small bear as if it were a large dog.

At one point my new Irish friend put his hand on the window glass, and the bear placed its paw on the other side of the glass opposite his hand as if it were attempting to make contact with an alien species. Then the bear casually lumbered around to the driver's side, stood on its hind legs, and leaned on the car. Oh for the days when I drove an automobile that a large animal could scrape its claws across at will, and produce no anxiety in me! The playful creature stood roughly 4 1/2 feet tall, and it was incredible to experience wildlife like this. The atmosphere was electric, yet peaceful. There was no traffic whatsoever as we lingered.

This short foray into Canada was like a scouting mission that prompted several future trips into the wilderness by foot or canoe. Like an addict, I craved getting away for more adventures. Due to a miraculous alignment of schedules, a friend at the lodge, Eric, and I had the same afternoon and following day off. Immediately after work we escaped into Canada like a couple of convicts, along with his 11-week-old golden retriever puppy, Briggs, and headed for Sleeping Giant. I wanted to experience the very soul of the park this time.

We decided to attempt hiking around most of the peninsula during our full day off, and positioned ourselves for a fast start the night before. We needed to be back to work at 7 a.m. the morning following this day off, so this didn't involve the best planning, to say the least. The journey started out splendidly, and included a cleansing swim in an uncharacteristically warm, shallow, sandy bay that was reminiscent of the Caribbean. This was mid-week, and with no one around for miles we were free to swim in our undies.

After this we climbed back onto the sleeping giant's chest, and quickly were caught over our heads as a violent thunderstorm broke out. We waited it out under a sheet of plastic, which was the only extra gear we had brought along besides water bottles! In exhaustion we slept in wet clothes on the trail after hiking 32 miles that day. The sleeping was brutal that night. I snuggled with Briggs, and he served as a heat pump.

Due to our poor planning, we didn't think the journey around the peninsula would be nearly that far. To arrive for work on time we set a watch for 4:30 a.m. so we could make it back to the car in the wee hours for the morning commute to work across the international border and two and a half hours of travel. The following morning we were shocked to find the car only a short stroll of perhaps a mile from where we bivouacked. Pitch-black darkness had descended ominously the night before. In our exhaustion the distance may as well have been 100 miles. Hurrying back to the lodge a bit late, we were within ten minutes of our start times, and had one rough day at the office!

My need to experience the undulations of the land bordered on the compulsive, and yet my character was blooming as the old insecurities faded away. If my work schedule had me working the afternoon shift in the restaurant at 2 or 3 pm, rather than sit around whiling away the time, I was busy hiking ten to fifteen miles, and would arrive at work just in the nick of time. If I was somewhat late it was difficult for the kind manager to be angry with me. My face beamed with a joyful ebullience akin to the face of Moses glowing from being in the presence of the glory of God when he descended from the mount after receiving the Ten Commandments.

It was most difficult when my trips didn't involve defined loops, but required turning around at some arbitrary point. One morning, for example, my good friend John and I biked from Cascade Lodge up the Gunflint Trail 50 to 60 miles one way. John hadn't had much exposure to wilderness yet. Due to the changes I was experiencing in myself, introducing friends to the wilderness became a remarkable passion. When we realized there was no hope of turning around and completing more than a hundred miles to punch the time clock in the early afternoon, we continued to press ahead until we reached a resort where we hoped we could purchase lunch and use the phone. By an amazing stroke of luck, when we called work our friend Eric answered the phone. He immediately agreed to shuttle us back to work with the Lodge pickup truck.

One evening, Mags and I joined Eric on a naturalist outing he led for the Lodge. I had an enormous crush on Mags, who spoke in a delightful Irish brogue, but was content to settle for a brother/sister-type relationship. On this particular evening I relished seeing two moose in a river that led to Northern Lights Lake, because it was her first encounter with the majestic creatures. At one point a beaver plied the waters in front of the canoe, two moose grazed in the river vegetation a scant 50 yards away, fish jumped here and there, and the sun settled down into a notch on the western horizon. Everyone was silent as we took in the majesty of the moment for a full half hour.

I'll share one last experience from the summer, and could go on and on with such tales. These adventures seemed to erupt volcanically into my life, helped change me, and the sheer exertion of the near-frenetic activity gradually readied my mind and spirit for something deeper and calmer.

Eric's cousin Jesse, a somewhat directionless kid contemplating dropping out of high school, ventured all the way from the state of Washington to visit. On a free afternoon, I volunteered to take him on an amazing hike to one of my favorite places, Eagle Mountain. At 2,301 feet, it is the highest point in Minnesota. Positioned in the Boundary Waters Canoe Area Wilderness, it offers a commanding view to the west of lakes, streams, and endless forest. There are no signs of civilization up there, and I beamed with pride as Jesse took in the fabulous landscape. Coming down from the "mountain," I saw three heads in the waters of charming little Whale Lake.

At first we took them to be ducks, and after we realized they were moose I dropped my bag, got my camera ready, and ran as fast as I could for a beach toward which they appeared to be aiming. Just 200 yards down the trail, perhaps half the distance to my goal, I heard loud splashing to my left and stopped in my tracks. A medium-sized cow moose stood in stunned silence, wearing the same expression of surprise and fear, just five feet away. She had two calves with her, so I greatly feared being charged as I remained frozen as a stone. Suddenly she jumped into the water in panic, her two calves awkwardly followed, and they swam back across the lake.

While reveling in the adrenaline and euphoria, we watched the young family for a short time until we realized we were covered in biting flies. We were so close to the water's edge that the cloud of deer and horse flies had migrated from the animals to us after they plunged back into the water. There were thousands of them. They were so thick that I couldn't even see Jesse's back through the swarm as they covered every square centimeter of real estate. It was like a scene taken from a killer bee movie. I cannot fathom how the beasts of the forests can handle such an onslaught all day long. As we sprinted back up the trail in frenzied hysteria we came across a porcupine waddling in the same direction. Our flight path carried us around the animal, and it seemed as if the beasts of the forest were all fleeing the same forest fire. Real adventure and discovery often do not begin until adversity strikes in some way.

16

EDUCATION OF A WANDERING MAN

That summer of discovery was fruitful in every way: mental, physical, spiritual. Body, mind, and soul connected in unique ways. Previously the different aspects of life were a jumble of isolated competing parts, much like the piles of random belongings in my childhood home. Understanding supplanted confusion. Equilibrium displaced imbalance. Peace overwhelmed anxiety and insecurity. Contentment flooded the wasteland of want. Love ambushed a heart that hitherto had merely been a mechanical pump that kept my body on life support.

Reading an autobiographical work by Louis L'Amour entitled *Education of a Wandering Man* reinforced a yearning to continue a path of education through travel and books. I had already learned far more during this short season than I gained in the formal college setting of the previous year. However, I was still on the fence over whether or not I should return to the well-worn path of institutional learning as the busy tourist season wound down and Labor Day approached. College is something that virtually everyone takes for granted. There is tremendous pressure to stay the course.

Reading *A Walk Across America*, by Peter Jenkins, tipped the scale and produced a confidence that enabled me to buck the system. His story was similar to mine in that he was disenchanted with society, and more importantly, with himself. He set off on a journey across America in an effort to find himself. Through the journey he succeeds in pulling off a trifecta in wondrous self-discovery, finding God, and meeting his wife. The reading of the story was a fantastic adventure. A world of possibilities unfurled that had nothing to do with the expectations of parents or society. One night of reading the book, above Partridge Falls on Labor Day weekend, was particularly memorable.

I stumbled upon this picturesque spot at the top of the continental United States by chance. I had been driving back roads in Grand Portage, Minnesota. Eventually I steered the car north for a bumpy drive on Partridge Falls Road, which is unmaintained and better suited for a four-wheel-drive vehicle. Luckily it was dry, so I cautiously wheeled my Honda Accord up the bumpy and rocky path fairly easily with a minimal loss of paint from the branches that constantly scraped the sides of the vehicle. Twenty minutes down the road brought me to the river, and the end of the line. Hearing the roar of the falls from the car, I rushed down the quarter-mile trail with great expectations.

The falls and the whole scene are picturesque beyond

description. Here I am on the day before Labor Day, and there wasn't a single human being to be found for miles at what I maintain is the most beautiful waterfall in Minnesota. The water plunges 50 feet into a nice gorge, and while there are other falls more than twice that size along the North Shore of Lake Superior, this one is more stunning than the rest. Perhaps this is due to its utter seclusion and the unlikelihood of seeing anybody there, the fact that Canada sits on the other side, or the lack of any modern safety features like railings or asphalt paths. Partridge Falls provides an enriching experience, and not just a photo-op. The portage and campsite all look the way they did when voyageurs and natives used it. This I find thrilling.

Since I had taken to traveling with a sleeping bag in the trunk of the car, just in case, I rolled it out near the top of the falls under old-growth white pines. This time I brought along a companion in Briggs, my roommate's golden retriever. He scouted out territory downstream and deep into the woods as it got dark, while I comfortably read *A Walk Across America* by the light of the fire in complete satisfaction. Everything was perfect. Lying there at the top of the United States, it seemed that the whole world fit snugly into the small of my back for support.

Feeling fully settled in, I stifled panic while hearing strange noises in the deep, dark forest. After I shined my headlamp in the general direction of the disturbance, it appeared that a bear on a ledge had casually lumbered off. A couple minutes later, unable to relax, I again shined my light toward this portal that seemed to be materializing my fears. The glowing orange eyes were still there! This time the animal was moving its head back and forth like a large cat. I was certain that it must be a cougar preying on me. I called Briggs, but he failed to appear. I knew he must be on his way, because he always came when called. Time stood still as the creature stared me down. Finally, I began packing up to leave.

At that moment the beast leaped off the ledge, charging toward me, and was about to pounce. Frantically I scanned the ground for something, anything, to fight it off with, but found NOTHING! At the last second, before imminent doom, I realized it was only Briggs. Phew. A light rain started to fall, and I happily used this as a pretext to relocate to a tiny abandoned shack at the end of the road, near the river. It wasn't much, but the roof kept us dry. More importantly, the four walls kept out mythical creatures on the prowl.

I spent the morning of Labor Day above the large falls reading and writing letters, which was my chief form of communication with the outside world. These were my press releases announcing my decision to not return to school for the upcoming term. This is a far more enjoyable way to notify parents of a controversial decision than to engage in arguments over the phone.

Suddenly, as if an apparition or vision, an elderly couple appeared. I was astonished to see people in the secluded setting, but welcomed them into my kingdom. The gentleman was a fascinating kindred spirit. He had worked as a U.S. customs agent back in the 1940s at the original border crossing where old US Highway 61 formerly crossed the river downstream. He talked of extreme winters, 30-foot snow drifts on either side of the road, moose, and life with the

Border Patrol at the remote entry to our country. A mere ten minutes of pleasantries resulted in a friendship rooting in my heart that continues to provide comfort and shade 20 years later, though the man is likely dead by now.

The experience capped off the short adventure perfectly, which was emblematic of what I sought on my travels. There was adventure, discovery of a new favorite place (of which there were many), an element of danger, solitude, exercise of the mind through reading and writing, a calm spirit, and an encounter with an interesting person. I needed all of these. The cool waters of solitude in particular can be tricky to navigate. Sometimes you reach the edge of the waters and are repulsed by your own reflection. To really appreciate and benefit from it, one must slip into the waters and allow them to roll over all of you—body, mind, spirit. And yet, solitude must be joined with a connection to humanity at some point. The two paradoxically fit hand-in-glove with one another, and allow for relations with each to flourish.

After this I had to see the former border crossing for myself. The bridge is now gone, but a Canadian flag proudly waves the red maple leaf on the other side. The old cabins that the customs agents formerly resided in continue to stand, and an older woman lived alone at the site. Stopping to allow all my senses to soak in the atmosphere, as if luxuriating in an Epson bath, I had a pleasant conversation with her. She kept a radio to call in any unusual activity to the Border Patrol, such as illegal river crossings, and I learned she was a writer of children's books. She recalled one experience of inviting three wet strangers to drink tea and warm themselves beside her wood stove while stalling them long enough to allow the

Border Patrol to arrive and arrest them. The area is completely isolated with no services whatsoever. The road isn't even maintained. It's incredible that an old woman could live on her own out there.

Later that day while toiling at work, still the holiday, I scraped copious amounts of food from the plates of wasteful and hurried tourists as a dishwasher in the restaurant. I had become accustomed to remarkably full days that abounded in such contrasts.

Immediately after finishing *A Walk Across America* I confidently walked into the office of the lodge owner, Gene Gladder, attempting to give my two weeks' notice. Though the leaves were turning on the trees, I casually informed him that I was planning on walking to Colorado. To add even more nonsense to the speech, I said I believed that God himself actually wanted me to do this. The absolute stunned confusion on Gene's face was palpable, because I had only recently committed to staying on at the restaurant through the winter as a waiter. I also had just signed a lease with a roommate, and moved into a cabin on a lake a short distance from the Gunflint Trail (a 63-mile-long road that penetrates deep into the wilderness and serves as one of the main gateways into the Boundary Waters Canoe Area Wilderness for eager travelers). With fifteen words attempting to escape his mouth at once, he stuttered considerably before emphatically stating, "Eddy, God does not want you to WALK to Colorado!" Thankfully the man talked some sense into me, and I left the meeting promising to think it over.

Ultimately I stayed at the restaurant, living up to the lease at the nice little cabin, and experienced the most rewarding season of my life. Gene agreed to allow me a five-week leave of absence in November and early December when tourism slows to a standstill prior to reliable snowfall. I planned on taking a larger-than-life road trip during that time. Afterward I hoped to hunker down in the quiet cabin, while working limited hours at the restaurant, until returning to college in March.

My cabin on Devil's Track Lake was rather close to Eagle Mountain via back roads. It served as a springboard for many fantastic experiences by providing quick access to several areas that allowed day trips into fairly remote wilderness. Adventures were abundant whether I roamed the backwoods or stayed in the cabin. Both were equally appealing. Books and letters followed me everywhere. They filled my pockets, backpacks, and car, so as to be available whenever I needed them whether planned or unplanned. A several-hour wait in a dirty mechanic's shop, for example, became a portal into other worlds and ideas. I was thriving as life gradually slowed down. Though much of my time was spent alone, loneliness became a relic of the past.

17

THE PIGEON

"The Pigeon" changed my life. First God, and now a mysterious "pigeon!" No, I don't claim to speak to the animals. At least I wouldn't admit to such a thing. Rather, The Pigeon is an ancient abandoned shack named after the river that proudly flows before it—whose name was derived from the now-extinct passenger pigeons that previously flocked in the area by the hundreds of thousands.

The Pigeon River drains much of the water from the Boundary Waters Canoe Area Wilderness (BWCA) that flows east to Lake Superior. Its richness contains the blood and mystique of voyageurs, explorers, and Native Americans that plied its waters for hundreds of years in one of the most important waterways in the entire world. It served as the gateway to the Great Northwest.

This was true adventure, because it not only quickened all five senses, but enlivened my imagination. The combination of risk, mystery, and a great story stoked my excitement and imprinted the discovery of The Pigeon on my psyche forever.

On a dreary rainy day in July 1995, I set out from the historic Grand Portage National Monument, which is located on what is now the Grand Portage Indian Reservation. Even though it was raining I could wait no longer, for the area seemed to call out to me. This seemingly insignificant spot marking the start of a hiking trail largely devoid of any impressive scenery is of enormous historical significance, being the inland headquarters of the British North West Company in the latter portion of the 18th century. Grand Portage was a location well known throughout the United States and Europe at that time, because it was the conduit through which most of the furs coming out of the entire northwestern portion of North America funneled to Lake Superior. All the furs had to pass down the nine-mile Grand Portage trail, which was necessary to bypass the numerous impassable rapids and waterfalls that beset the last 21 miles of the river as it races to the great lake. A significant stockade sat on the Lake Superior side of the portage, the location of each wooden picket painstakingly located in the current structure's reproduction of the original.

From there the furs—predominately beaver pelts—were shipped by large canoes through the Great Lakes to Montreal, where they were exported to London for processing into fashionable hats for the wealthy. Various styles of top hats, such as the kind Abraham Lincoln was later famous for wearing, were particularly popular. The cost was exorbitant, to say the least. In addition to the numerous lives lost among the ranks of voyageurs, the fashion item commanded a price equal to six months wages for the average worker.

Though the fur trade was marked by exorbitant wealth and greed, it was the impetus for exploration during this period. Much of history was shaped, not by wars, but by means of the trading network that extended thousands of miles along waterways throughout the continent. It was the age of exploration of North America as voyageurs paddled waters great and small by canoe throughout the Northwest to and from distant fur-trading outposts as far away as Lake Athabasca some 2,000 miles away. These seemingly fearless men were only limited by the roughly five months available for travel between May and October when the lakes were thawed. Much of the border between Canada and Minnesota was determined by using the route these voyageurs travelled as a superhighway to reach northern destinations, where the best beaver furs could be found. The Treaty of Paris, following the American Revolution, placed the international boundary between the newly formed United States and British North America along the line of water communication between Lake Superior and Lake of the Woods.

On their canoe route, now called the border route, travelers today carry their canoes across the same portages the voyageurs used while carrying their heavy loads between the lakes. A few lob pines still mark the route across large lakes, and locations of portages and campsites. These were large prominent pines from which the voyageurs had lobbed off central branches, rendering the tree naked in the middle, so that it could be sighted for miles across open water.

The exact boundary between the nations was under dispute for years until the Webster-Ashburton Treaty of 1842 specifically fixed the border along the Pigeon River and the Height of Land Portage between North and South Lakes. This particular portage was considered the true entry point by the voyageurs, and is steeped in lore. All men passing this way were to be initiated by a baptism ceremony, thus equalizing the rich and poor alike at this hallowed location for a brief moment, after which one was officially recognized as a Nor-Wester (or North man). I too went through a similar ceremony in which I stood knee deep in the Canadian waters of North Lake as water was sprinkled on my head and face by a cedar bough. An oath was then recited, as was done by countless luminaries in the past, to never allow a new hand to cross this same spot without going through this ceremony, and to never kiss a voyageur's wife without her permission. Someday I'll bring my own kids to partake in the same tradition. Gazing north from the beach at North Lake into Canada toward the great Northwest is exhilarating due to the mystique of this famous location and the many famed individuals and explorers that passed through and partook in this ritual.

A simple marker defines the exact location of the border, and one may cheerfully hop from one side to the other. In addition to passing between the countries, this short portage crosses the Laurentian Divide, which separates the watersheds of the Atlantic and Arctic Oceans. On the Canadian side the waters flow north to Hudson Bay, while the waters south drain to the Atlantic Ocean via Lake Superior and the St. Lawrence Seaway.

Even deep in the wilderness history can touch you like a match to a fuse, and spark your imagination. The voyageurs, and some knighted explorers who journeyed with them on occasion, were in the vanguard of the settlement of the continent. I was enthralled with explorers like Sir Alexander Mackenzie, who repeatedly passed through Grand Portage. Mackenzie completed the first east to west crossing of North America a full ten years prior to Lewis and Clark's famous expedition. The many tales of these brave individuals resonated with my own urge to explore new country.

Two years after this first hike of the Grand Portage, for example, I worked at the Grand Portage National Monument as a park ranger-interpreter for the National Park Service. I was issued authentic-looking voyageur clothing. Not even one full day after receiving this attire I had my first free weekend, and decided to sport my new threads on my first solo canoe trip into the BWCA. I was dressed as a voyageur from head to toe in the lake country that I immensely loved. Getting off to a late start that first night, I missed my first portage off a large lake due to darkness and possible ineptitude. Still being outside the BWCA, I knocked on a cabin door to obtain permission to make camp at the water's edge. A pair of honeymooners from the big city opened the door to discover me standing there in my full regalia at nearly 10 p.m. What a sight that must have been!

Leaving well before dawn the next day, I easily found my portage while paddling placid water as smooth as glass. Loons called, birds sang gloriously, and the costumed paddler effortlessly glided in the stern of a canoe through a light fog. The atmosphere was magical for this wannabe voyageur. I crossed the first short portage, and entered into the designated wilderness. The lake was rather small, possessing a long and narrow shape like an exclamation mark. It was a remarkably calm morning, and the lake was absolutely still. I gently placed the canoe into the water, and set the tip of the stern on the rocky beach before running back down the trail to retrieve my belongings. I returned with my backpack a short time later, and discovered in horror that I was marooned. The canoe had drifted far into the lake. What previously looked like a large pond, suddenly seemed like a Great Lake!

I removed my leather mukluk-like footwear, walked through the muck, and reluctantly plunged into the cold waters to begin a swim of desperation while heavily laden with my clothes. The pants were especially thick and cumbersome, and my feet functioned as nearly useless tiny flippers. It seemed like I was hardly moving while gauging my progress with the land and with the canoe that continued to drift farther out into the deeps. Finally, in complete exhaustion, I reached the life-saving canoe. However, I was so sapped of energy that I found it completely impossible to climb into the tippy boat. I futilely kicked toothpick-like legs that culminated in what seemed like stubs, my worthless dwarf feet, and powered the vessel like a paddleboat as I pushed the 16 feet of canoe from the stern toward the distant shore. The total distance may have been 200 yards, but it felt like a mile as the interminable workout dragged on forever and drained every remaining ounce of energy. At times I studied logs along the shore and seemed to lose ground against the current. Finally I made it back, and thus lived to tell the tale, salvaging the rest of what turned out to be a pleasant weekend. I nearly drowned during the ordeal, and learned that one should remove clothing prior to swimming deep into a lake. Such a basic lesson could save your life one day. Properly securing a canoe is another.

All this, and I could go on for an entire book, is meant to state that the Grand Portage is aptly named. It wasn't just a hiking trail to me. It was, and is, so much more. On this rainy July day I embarked down the nine-mile portage with the attitude and heart of an intrepid explorer on a date with destiny. By the time I reached the end of the portage I was drenched and frozen from heavy rains, splattered by mud, covered in mosquito bites, and yet remained in high spirits. I was at the site of the old Fort Charlotte on the Pigeon River side of the portage, and hadn't seen another soul. It was the first time I had hiked to the Canadian border, and this exact location was rich with history and chronicled in the journals of many important figures. For someone with an adventurous heart, it doesn't get much better than this. Later, having been shown what to look for as a park ranger, I would have eyes to see the scant remains of the old fort. On my first visit, however, my imagination more than adequately filled in the details.

After basking in the stories of old, the geographical significance of the site, and dreaming of being a new explorer journeying into the great unknown up the Pigeon River, I headed back. I then took a detour down an unmaintained mucky trail about a mile long to see the cascades, which promised to provide more interesting scenery. The series of three spectacular waterfalls cutting into a deep gorge did not disappoint. There were no human footprints whatsoever.

Only bear, deer, and moose tracks stood out as I imagined being the first to set foot on this untrammeled territory.

The river rushes violently into a chasm in ancient Canadian Shield rock and narrows within a deep gorge that reaches a depth of perhaps 75 feet or more at its deepest point. I threw several rocks into Canada. My imagination went wild for several years when pondering the origins of a flat wooden structure that seemed older than time, which rested immediately above the cauldron of the cascades. With a little more courage or foolishness, for often the two are bedfellows, I could have walked over it into Canada. Some years later, after most of the structure was washed away by the swollen river during an exceptionally powerful spring runoff, I came across an old picture from around the 1920s that showed this to be the remains of a sluice used to divert floating logs (destined for Lake Superior where they were floated down the lake in large rafts) around the cascades from lumber operations upstream.

The Canadian side of the river possesses remarkable topography with very large hills, rocky outcroppings, and great beauty. No sign of human activity is visible throughout the field of view that spans many miles and portions of two nations. I explored up and down the river as time permitted, but it was imperative to make it back to the car by nightfall. Eventually, while becoming nearly hypothermic due to exposure to cold rain the entire day and from trudging through wet brush, I stumbled upon an old abandoned cabin. More than likely it was some sort of foreman's shack from the logging days. The door was unlocked, and I was astonished to discover that it is free for anybody to use (who can find it).

The growing shadows of the day only allowed me to spend an hour relaxing in the cabin. Though the time was short, it was magical and life-changing.

I was exhausted from the experience, and gratefully soaked in warmth from the fire I built in the ancient woodstove. It dried me out considerably, and left me feeling warm and toasty. The break from the hordes of biting insects was also a welcome respite. Several journals chronicled the most recent 30 years of visitor history, and carvings in the walls showed casual use dating to the 1960s. A pair of luxurious wool socks hung invitingly on the clothesline, and my pruned feet snuggled deeply into them. Never before or since have I been so grateful for warm socks! I still have them twenty years later. Pulling the scratchy old pair over weary metatarsals brings sweet memories.

Wishing I had a sleeping bag to pass the night before returning to work in the morning, I reluctantly hauled myself out of there around 7 or 8 p.m. as the sun dropped uncomfortably low in the sky. I still had a journey of nine miles before me, but at least the rain had ceased. Great armies of mosquitoes came out with a vengeance following the precipitation. I ran the entire way back in my clunky hiking boots, stopping only to pee (which was agony with enormous clouds of thousands of mosquitoes enveloping and puncturing me). Try not urinating on yourself while frantically swatting them in such conditions!

Ravenous as a horse, I returned to my car and civilization in complete darkness. I had only packed a single granola bar, but thrilled in what had been an amazingly fulfilling day that greatly exceeded my already elevated expectations. Hiking back to such remote scenery, rather than driving to an overlook conveniently located along a highway, brought tremendous satisfaction. Additionally, while I only had solitude as a companion on this trip through time and space, I never felt alone. It was as if God was walking with me the entire way, sharing in the adventure. What a contrast to my sorry existence just a couple months prior when I despaired in loneliness after even a short spell alone. I never would have embarked on a 20-mile journey like this by myself prior to this. The sense of desolation, abandonment, friendlessness, and complete emptiness would have overwhelmed me. It is impossible to adequately underscore how freeing it was to be liberated from always minding the opinions of others, and being chained to their idea of fun.

18

ENDURING INFLUENCE OF THE PIGEON

The Pigeon is timeless. It looks the same today as it did when I discovered it in another century, a full two decades ago.

The place left such an impression on me that I returned to the humble cabin another half dozen times or more over the course of the next eight months. It became my new home away from home. Today I write these lines in a room above my garage that I created out of an attempt to re-create the feeling of this dwelling that has been such a positive influence. I sit in silence here as the woodstove chugs along with a new fire crackling and gaining steam. Before me are walls paneled in 100-year-old boards salvaged from an old garage so as to resemble an ancient cabin. My blackened fingers appear to have been grappling with coal due to fiddling with my first fire of the season on a cold, rainy, late summer day. Here I am able to conjure up memories of The Pigeon any time I wish. More importantly, I slow down and take on the mindset of the cabin. This place isn't simply about memories of the past. Rather, it's an alternative way of being. I am able to more fully live in the present. More intentionally. With focus. Clarity.

Fall is a magnificent time to visit the cabin. Deer flies, horse flies, black flies, mosquitoes, and an army of ticks—thousands upon thousands of them so intent on stealing away with a morsel of flesh or drilling down to warm blood—have either returned to dormancy or are too busy rotting away in the soil to be a bother. Huge hills in Canada, boasting rocky outcroppings like great battlements, light up in a conflagration of brilliant colors. Looking across the chasm of the river at the fascinating Canadian topography presents a panorama of brilliant reds, oranges, yellows, and the greens of conifers interspersed throughout. While there, one is nearly assured of coming across no sign of other people. Even the sounds of civilization (such as airplanes or distant snowmobiles) are extremely rare. The solitude of the wilderness is complete.

Other than the passing transitions of the seasons, it is a place that hardly changes. I've come to appreciate the predictable environment that remains there. Every time I arrive is like returning to Grandma and Grandpa's house. The cabin, forest, river, hills, and silence are always there, dependable as bedrock. Even now, I'm comforted knowing this rich environment awaits my next return. I can picture individual trees within the scrubby forest, scant remnants of old growth timber that escaped the logger's axe, rocky outcrops, the bend of the river, the moose antlers and skull that have hung over the door for ages, ancient animal traps dangling on the outside wall facing north along the entryway (yes, men have been the primary decorators), and the view of the sunset while gazing west up the river.

One tree stands out in particular, and I don't believe I'll ever locate it again. While in college, I returned to this place several times each year. I was so accustomed to the rigors of the journey that I took them for granted, forgetting that my untested travel companions were often on maiden voyages. One late fall evening found my friend Mike and me crashing through the last mile of brush in utter darkness. The trail was often indecipherable in daylight, so in the darkness I resorted to aiming in the general direction. For some odd reason I didn't rely on a compass. My heart and mind felt a strong magnetic pull to the place, and I preferred to rely on "feel." I do not recommend this "method" to anyone. After spending 20 minutes on a circuitous route, I howled in delight upon stumbling across an enormous white pine, which is highly uncharacteristic of the brushy forest there. In excitement and glee I exclaimed to Mike, "I've NEVER seen this amazing tree before. It must be five or six feet in diameter!" Of course this immediately gave away the fact that I didn't have a bearing on our exact location, and was cause for some degree of panic in my friend. He sought the assistance of the Almighty as we bowed our heads, and soon we were back on the right path and firmly ensconced in the comfort of the candle-lit cabin. Despite numerous attempts at locating the impressive pine in the years that followed, I have been unable to catch a glimpse of the behemoth since that remarkably dark evening.

Inside the cabin resides a pockmarked table adorned with decades of carvings of names and designs that are often filled with candle wax. A ten-inch-high pile of journals rests on the table, providing weight to the place. The journals anchor the cabin into a fascinating history shared by many grateful visitors over the decades. Without them the dwelling would perhaps devolve into nothing more than four walls and a roof. A deck of playing cards and an ancient cribbage board add further amusement and activity to the rustic table that is the center of all entertainment, visiting, and meals. Above the table, comprising much of the western wall of the shack, is a large picture window. Completing the western wall is a pair of bunk beds with nothing but springs upon which to lay your foam pad and sleeping bag.

Tradition relegates all newcomers, regardless of social status, to the top bunk for their first night so they may experience the full heat of the inferno-prone woodstove. It graces the southern wall, resting just three feet from the bunks. When a very large individual sinks into the top bunk they may sag down 18 inches at the bottom of their rump. Years of pleasant evenings in the cabin, however, make me trust that the metal springs will hold.

The woodstove can be virtually impossible to regulate properly, and naturally one wants to fill it with wood prior to turning in at night. It is not uncommon for everyone (two people sleeping on the bunks and two on the floor) to wake up simultaneously in terror due to a tsunami-like wave of heat that has engulfed and overrun the place. The sight of the newcomer in nothing but a pair of boxers hugging the exterior wall for any relieving cooler temperature is cause for amusement.

Once, four of us shot out of the cabin in our underwear due to temperatures that were more suited to a steamy sauna. I believe it must have exceeded 150 degrees. On each side of the picture window are candleholders. Due to extreme heat, the tapered candles had softened to the point that they bent downward in an upside-down J. This was the middle of the night, and they had been unlit. Our solution was to shovel snow into the woodstove as railroad men formerly heaved coal into the firebox. Soon we fell asleep on top of our sleeping bags wearing a minimum of clothing for just the barest sense of human decency. We later awoke to temperatures somewhere around freezing in the shack. The character of individuals staying in the cabin can largely be judged based upon how they handle and react to this kind of adversity. One is guaranteed struggle of some kind while deep in this wilderness. Those who are patient and cheerful in withstanding such trials are generally the sort that become close friends. Hardship peels away one's exterior, revealing what a man is made of. Such shared experiences forge lasting relationships.

Despite the difficulties the big woodstove presents, it has always been the ideal stove in my mind. It is a large barrel that was long ago converted to a wood burner, so we refer to it as a barrel stove. Very long logs, perhaps three feet long, can be tossed into it, which saves time on firewood collection. The metal of the stove is becoming thin, and the sides glow bright red when a good fire gets to crackling. Someday we'll have to figure out a way to replace the aging barrel. The door, with the letters FOK emblazoned upon it, is thick cast iron. The entire unit possesses a well-used rusty patina. The high-pitched creaking sound of the door swinging open is music to my ears. It is one of the first things you hear upon arriving in exhaustion after enduring frigid temperatures well below zero and completing at least half the journey in darkness. After the fire is lit there's a bit of a wait for the real heat to come, and then you'll hear the telltale "tick tick tick" sound from the metal of the groaning stove and pipe as it really gets going. Then you know to prepare for the sweltering that is to come.

Behind and to the left of the stove is a large pile of firewood. It has to be big, because of the junk wood being burned. It is good etiquette for those staying in The Pigeon to leave behind a nice pile of wood that reaches a height of about 40 inches and spans four feet in width. This is very important. It is common for the remarkably weary traveller to arrive in the middle of the night in winter. I've often arrived at midnight or later in temperatures of -20°F or colder in January with a beard thoroughly encrusted in ice, and toes experiencing the beginnings of frostbite.

My last experience at the cabin saw the mercury plunge down to the upper 20s below zero. There was so much fresh snow that I had a huge problem of snow getting into my ski boots and melting down into my socks. I was careless in not bringing gaiters to seal the opening. I had extreme difficulty pulling my boots off because my socks were frozen to the bottoms. All feeling was lost in my toes. My friend Zach and I had skied in through fresh powder that was beyond four feet deep in the woods. I was feeling exhausted and uncharacteristically cold at the halfway point on this particular journey. Normally the workout is so strenuous that only extremities may experience some cold. The experience was a good reminder of the importance of skiing in with a friend. He tossed me an energy bar that perked me right up until we reached our destination.

Numerous poplar thickets were so encumbered by the weight of snow that they bent down over the trail into hellacious tangles to be navigated. This would be relatively simple in the summer, but it becomes hell on earth to do so on skis with a heavy backpack containing a sleeping pad protruding horizontally from both sides of the load. Hell on earth is not an overstatement. It is also frequently necessary to pass beneath downed trees that force you to stick your nose right down into the snow as you just barely clear the underside of the tree that steadfastly blocks passage. Other times you may engage in the trick of passing over the tree if it rests close enough to the surface of the snow, but this can also be a trick due to the presence of branches and the height to be cleared while wearing five-foot-long skis and being uneasily balanced under a burdensome pack.

And yet, winter is far and away the best time of year to visit the cabin. While most of the world dreams of visiting the Bahamas this time of year, I long to return to The Pigeon with my friends.

Due to the shortened days it is inevitable to complete a portion of the journey on an unpacked soft trail under cover of darkness. In the dark it easily takes twice as long for some reason, and this is even true when a full moon allows for travel through the bright white landscape without the aid of a flashlight. It is not uncommon for the trip to take five or six hours even though we only need to travel six miles due to parking on a secret unmaintained road that shaves three miles off my original route. Experienced skiers who have joined us find it impossible to believe that a mere six miles could take six hours, but later discover this to be the case. One has to endure the struggle for themselves to believe it.

By the time I come across the well-known shadows outlining the presence of the cabin in the dark forest, and hear the sounds of the Pigeon River, I have sometimes been so grateful upon arrival that I could nearly cry. If I was alone I probably would. The snow piles high outside the door, which swings in when you remove the stick that serves as a lock in the latch. The appearance of the interior of the cabin is always exactly as you remember it. I stare longingly at the woodstove as a weary traveler gazes at an oasis with its life-preserving water. It is also incredibly relieving to find nobody else inside, which after 50 or more trips, has only happened twice. Stepping down into this place of repose from the ample snowpack, which has been the epicenter of much personal growth and reflection, the first thing you do is take off your heavy burden and light a fire in the FOK stove. Never have you been so grateful for shelter and warmth. Believe me. Then one turns to lighting candles and making the place a home for the next couple days by laying out sleeping bags and unpacking.

Half of the east side of the cabin is taken up by a useful working counter. Above this a cupboard houses decades of filth along with odds and ends people have left behind as contributions to the cabin. Formerly there was an inspiring ancient oil lamp and numerous oddities that were fun to rifle through, but on occasion some of the more anal retentive among the Pigeon's users will clean out what they view as garbage from the recesses. The journal entry marks the occasion with a sharply worded lecture about keeping the cabin clean.

As the years have passed, the number of visitors to the cabin has dwindled to a die-hard trickle of just two to four groups per year. As many of these individuals increase in age, the numbers have dropped considerably. The small group of regulars who frequent the cabin share a bond of friendship, though most of us have never met. Communication with each other is made through the journals. Each entry is studied carefully since your previous visit, as if chronicling vital history. On a recent trip I was saddened to discover a precipitous drop of logs in the journal.

Heading north along the eastern wall you come to the windows that open by swinging in, which still have tattered screens intact. The space between the screens and windowpanes make a nice freezer. All perishable food is stuffed here, remaining frozen solid until needed. It also serves as a handy cooler for the precious and tremendously refreshing few bottles of beer hauled in. Rounding out this end of the cabin is a closet that is best avoided due to mouse activity, but it does contain useful axes and saws for the all-important duty of replenishing the woodpile.

There is a substantial amount of dead wood near the cabin, but due to the sizable snow pack, in the winter one often is required to venture out in order to find a standing dead tree that is suitable for felling. The men behave as boys pretending to be lumberjacks while engaging in this work. It can be a fantastically enjoyable sweat-breaking activity, and yet exhausting. Dropping the tree is the easy part, but chopping and sawing it into useful pieces takes perseverance. The stumps aren't noticeable in the winter, but summer and fall display a somewhat comical scene of three and four-foot-tall stumps littering the area.

The door sits on the northern side of the cabin, as it should. One exits the cabin facing Canada and the great north, toward the river, and all the hills beckoning on the Canadian side. This heightens the sense of adventure whenever the door alluringly opens. The exhilarating feeling strikes me even upon leaving the cabin to relieve myself in the middle of the night, or to fill the pot with snow to melt into drinking water atop the barrel stove.

Being outside the cabin on a cold, clear, crisp night below zero is wonderful. Often these quick trips outside are taken in nothing but slippers and a bright red union suit. I stand outside for a few minutes as if taking a break from a sauna. On clear nights the stars are astonishingly bright, with occasional wisps of clouds blowing over. The frigid temperatures cause a swelling of appreciation for the absolute luxury of the cabin. Sometimes the wind howls uproariously through the trees. By this time large icicles are forming from the roof of the cabin and hanging over the windows. Candlelight from within seeps out the windows between the icicles, casting a magical appearance. On especially cold nights at twenty to even forty degrees below zero, when there tends to be no wind, the smoke billowing from the chimney floats straight up to the heavens into the moonlight and dances among the stars. It is well worth the effort of tuning in for these enchanting episodes of Dancing With the Stars.

These are my favorite times at the cabin. There is no internal pressure to be out exploring. I can comfortably sit and read for hours in silence. When inviting friends it is important to encourage significant swaths of silence so everyone can experience the true gift of The Pigeon. This is often a challenge for my friends, but well worth the effort. There is still plenty of time for playing card games, horsing around, and hours spent in conversation, but cutting out useless chatter and noise is of paramount importance. The pilgrimage to this place builds lasting relationships. Nearly all my closest friendships have been built upon and cemented in shared experiences at this place that is unique among all the wonders of the world.

I think of my good friend John Baker, with whom I slogged in on snowshoes through the deepest powder I've ever seen. He was inexperienced and awkward atop a borrowed pair of large old-fashioned snowshoes. It became necessary for us to take turns shouldering a burdensome navy gunnysack, because he didn't have a fancy backpack. Those were eight of the longest hours of our lives, as we endured a trial that was every bit as much mental as it was physical.

Cheap cigars were especially sweet and satisfying at 2:00 am with him. Our trust in each other deepened remarkably as the conversation went on for hours about God, spiritual matters, and the meaning of life. Responsibilities at work forced us to return the next day, but the trip out took half the time on a packed path on a warm, sunny day. Twelve hours of gut-busting effort exchanged for half again that many hours awake in the cabin was well worth forging an alliance with a trusted friend that will last a lifetime.

John and I frequented several wilderness cabins that winter. This became our chief form of entertainment. These experiences are some of my most cherished memories, and usually involved enjoying silence together as we read books for hours, occasionally looking up to talk in intervals that often lasted only ten minutes. I learned that comfortable silences are one of the marks of a solid friendship.

At first I was reaching out to him, because he was a seemingly ambition-less young man disenchanted with life. I was changed and affected every bit as much as him, however. John worked as a low-level cook with bleak prospects in the restaurant. At one point as an 18-year-old, he lived in a trailer with a humungous eight-foot-wide satellite dish parked out front that cost him $2,500 to further his escape from reality in television. His gradual transformation was every bit as remarkable as my own.

Our cabin visits were often as short as three or four hours, the first hour spent just getting the interior up to a comfortable temperature. These shorter visits were enjoyed at cabins requiring short walks that ranged from 200 yards to a mile. Jim Korf's ramshackle shack—which blew apart into toothpicks during the blowdown storm of 1999 that produced winds in excess of 100 miles per hour—was located on private land on Birch Lake near the edge of the Boundary Waters about halfway up the Gunflint Trail. Now deceased, Jim was an eccentric artist who built the quirky cabin. He led a transient existence, and said we were free to use it, but that the owner of the property might not approve. Thus we snuck in at night, and were careful not to arouse attention. The one-room shack with a loft was filled with abandoned eccentricities, and if we were lucky enough to spend the night due to both of us having afternoon shifts in the restaurant the next day, the morning sun was particularly magical as it penetrated numerous windows. Jim had built one of these as a bird feeder that brought the birds into what felt like the interior of the cabin because it was recessed into the dwelling by a full three feet. The window opened so you could place food on the large shelf. It wasn't long before whiskey jacks came to retrieve the treasures.

These experiences certainly left their mark on John. His new faith flourished through them, and he wound up spending several years living in small one-room cabins that he rented for as little as $75 a month as he used a lifestyle influenced by Henry David Thoreau to gradually morph into a fascinating and deep person. His son's middle name is Thoreau, in fact. Getting to one cabin involved a long drive up a remote gravel road, followed by a hike in that was just long enough to warm you up on a cold day. Here his solitude was certainly more complete than Thoreau's even. On warm winter days the college dropout, who had attempted playing hockey at Hibbing Community College, ice-skated on a small pond he shoveled off for the purpose. Visiting him one windy evening with winds blasting below-zero air through the gaps around the door, I was stunned to discover the dwelling couldn't be heated beyond about 50 degrees by the undersized woodstove. John swears this was only a problem on the coldest nights. Of course there are many of these that close to the Canadian border.

The summer prior to taking up residence in the cabin, he lived an animal-like existence as a squatter atop a breezy hill at the end of a logging road in a small, old, and grubby trailer. He kept a red Coleman cooler buried in the dirt on the shady side around back, which was filled with nothing but Mountain Dew, bacon, and hot dogs. It was dry, sunny, and hot up there at the top of a recent clearcut. His nearest water source was a half-mile away in the swamp-like headwaters of the Cascade River, so he hauled in jugs of water from the hotel where he worked as a housekeeper. Hygiene was basic or non-existent. He got away with this arrangement for a few months, until the U.S. Forest Service chased him away.

I think of Mel, a party-animal college student who never stopped telling hilarious jokes and stories, and found it difficult to slow down to the pace of The Pigeon. In the middle of the night we bedded down right on the trail, laying sleeping bags on pads directly on the snow under the stars on a relatively mild evening a mile from the cabin. We were aware of travelers who weren't vacating the place until morning. Temperatures plummeted below zero overnight, and morning was supremely difficult as we forced tender feet into boots that were frozen stiff. Water bottles were frozen solid, and we were miserable as our company of three college students made our way through that last mile of brush to reach the destination. Today the man is a remarkably busy attorney with far too many responsibilities, and an ambition as wide as the horizon. Though I've gone years without seeing him, a recent surprise knock at my door provided the opportunity to pick up where we left off. This wouldn't have been possible without this one weekend of travails and triumphs.

The best man at my wedding, and enduring friend of 20 years even though he lives some distance away, would not be as close today if it weren't for The Pigeon. With six kids, he is probably the finest family man and one of the most active dads I know. He joins me on annual winter trips to the cabin, which provide splendid opportunities for us to catch up. Joining us are newer friends that continue to forge bonds with us through such experiences.

Generally we are content to laze around the cabin much of the day, having worked so hard to arrive, but we still rouse ourselves for fresh air and adventure. In earlier years, before heightened border security concerns, we crossed into Canada in ambitious attempts to climb the imagination-capturing hills in the distance, which always wound up being much farther away than they appeared. We became distracted with attempts at such things as capturing a ruffed grouse for dinner, or my personal favorite, pushing dead trees into the gorge. No worries here, Canadians; the rabble-rousing always remains in America now. I laugh like a little boy when we finally are successful in rocking large dead trees back and forth as they crash into the deep gorge from the precipice. We haven't lost a man yet from this somewhat reckless behavior.

The Pigeon has indelibly left its mark on me. Ample hours and days there helped remove the clutter of my life, and to integrate what had been a fragmented existence. It takes time, but gradually the warm silence peels away the detritus of the mind. I delight in sharing this lifestyle with others, and prefer that cell phones and other distractions be left behind. Clarity and focus come as the multi-tasking of the modern world is abandoned.

Since winter is the best season to enjoy the place, and my
friends and I all have families to tend to, we now try to
venture back to this paradise only once annually when deep
snow can generally be counted on. Skiing back to reality is
typically many times easier than the hard slog in.

Once we received 20 inches of beautiful powdery snow while
being safely ensconced in the silent backcountry. Dan, my
new friend Ryan, and I arrived back at the car to find the
road unplowed, as we feared would be the case. Though the
snow was of a light and fluffy consistency that lake-effect
snow often is, we found it impossible to coax my 1992 Honda
Accord station wagon up the steep hills. Per the suggestion of
my friends, who are committed family men, mind you, they
sat on the hood of the car to give it more weight up front. I
white-knuckled the steering wheel in terror at 40 miles per
hour, as Ryan hollered into a walkie-talkie to give it more gas
on the straightaway leading to a sizable hill that contained a
significant banked curve. They held onto the lip of the hood
below the windshield for their lives. Against my better
judgment I got the car up to 45 miles per hour on the fourth
or fifth try, with visions of my close friends being launched
from the hood as we spun out of control. Miraculously, we
made it over several steep hills and approximately five miles
of snowed-in conditions unscathed prior to reaching plowed
pavement. The experience was absolutely crazy, but
necessary for us all to return to civilization for jobs and
families. Each year the trip brings hardships worth writing
home about. For such reasons I now only venture back there
in the company of trusted friends, which once again has

provided me with the majority of my social network.

The Pigeon remains my ideal vacation spot, retreat to silence, and epicenter for camaraderie. For years I wanted to live in a tiny shack for at least a full winter, or even a lifetime, where I'd spend my time reading, writing, contemplating, exploring, and occasionally entertaining. Ultimately I chose a wife and family over this ideal, and was happy to do so. Prior to getting married I satisfied this itch somewhat by spending a week alone at a friend's cabin deep in the woods 50 miles north of Duluth, Minnesota, near the sparsely populated old Finnish settlement of Toimi. I enjoyed a pleasant week in mid-winter during a break in my senior year of college. I immersed myself in the world of Leo Tolstoy's amazing novel, *War and Peace*, engaged in various chores, and luxuriated daily in a genuine Finnish sauna, which, thanks to my friend Brandon, became a lifelong obsession.

The structure is over 100 years old, and is comprised of hand-hewn squared old-growth timbers. A fantastic woodstove graces the sauna—a sturdy barrel stove. It is more than capable of heating the room to the desirable temperature of 185°F and to uncomfortable temperatures beyond 200° even. Another barrel rests vertically, which is filled with water. The water naturally circulates without any kind of pump through pipes that run along the heated stove. This water is transformed thus, as if it were removed from the Fountain of Youth, and provides the most amazing bathing experience I've ever had. Shampoo and soap are slathered on generously. Sweat, grime, and suds are washed away with ladle after ladle of warm water, and followed by a douse of cold for a sense of minty freshness. I have never felt so clean as after emerging from this portal into Finnish culture to stand out in the snow wearing nothing but a smile as steam wafts from my bright red cooked-lobster-looking body in the frigid night air. On one or two occasions I have taken so many trips to the sauna that capillaries have burst in my chest. The resulting blotchy appearance whipped up the hypochondriac in me to the point that I was relieved to wake up alive the next day. Alas, even good things should be enjoyed in moderation...

Brandon grew up taking these saunas with his family, as his forefathers did, and thinks nothing of sitting naked with mother, father, and sisters. I admire the trust he has in his kin. It has helped make him into a father worthy of emulation.

This is a microcosm of what it is like to spend time in cabins deep in the woods. They leave you naked and bare, and can sometimes bring you to tears while showing you what kind of person you are without the masks so often worn when dwelling amidst civilization. Out there it is just you, your maker, the creatures of the forest, silence, along with your own thoughts and capacity for enjoying the stillness.

Cabin life is enjoyed by nearly everyone. This is due to its stripped-down minimalism that emphasizes the things that really matter to one's self. Possessions, clutter, busyness, and a frenetic lifestyle are all left behind. Being in tune and in touch with the natural world promotes true reflection that can lead to positive and lasting change in your life.

19

ALL ABOARD

In late October, a week prior to leaving on a highly anticipated road trip, I put my car into a ditch on Trout Lake Road while hurrying back to work after spending the night camping. The first snow of the season came that night, about four inches, and the winding gravel road was unforgiving. After sustaining a fair amount of damage to my trusty Honda, known as Madeline, I concluded that a trip by car spanning many thousands of miles across mountain ranges was not sensible. I had foolishly contemplated a jaunt up and down the Alaska-Canadian Highway to the 49th state. Alone, this late in the season, my date with the ditch was a "happy accident" that saved me from a potentially disastrous experience.

The next day I emerged from a travel agent's office with an All Aboard America pass from Amtrak for rail travel. In hand was a golden ticket that allowed me to circumnavigate the entire western half of the country over a period of 30 days for a mere $198. What an adventure this was, the climax of my furlough from the real world, an investment that continues to pay whopping dividends, and one of the best decisions I've ever made. The timing of the trip was perfect. I was still unsure of my future, whether or not to ever return to school, and eagerly pondered the direction of my life.

After visiting Mom at my childhood home south of Milwaukee, I boarded the train loaded for bear with freeze dried meals and oatmeal. Oh how she worried about me! She had returned from work a full hour later than planned, due to a last minute stop of panic-buying that procured more camp food than I could stuff in my pack. Looking out the window of the cluttered living room, I despaired that I was sure to miss my train. Suddenly, she came barreling in like a torpedo (only to be followed by a police officer who took his time writing her a hefty ticket). Amazingly, the train was an hour late in arriving, so I was able to catch it just in the nick of time. Burdened by a pack weighing 60 pounds (at the time I was a featherweight at a buck twenty), I hurried like a salmon swimming upstream against throngs of people heading away from the train platform. I caught the gleam of the kindly conductor's eyes as I shouted to announce my presence between asthmatic gasps of air while he was closing the door to the nearest railcar.

With a racing heartbeat and sweating bullets, I plopped down in a window seat feeling most fortunate. Only then did I have the opportunity to wave goodbye to Mom as I headed for the great unknown. Her tears bespoke fears that she'd never see me again. The bond of this single mother to her only child was the lens through which all things were seen. While I wasn't her all-in-all, reality certainly approached that level of totality.

The first stretch was from Milwaukee to West Glacier, Montana, so I had plenty of time (about 28 hours) to read, write, and observe. From the start I was drawn to an African American man who was a passionate evangelist. He spoke of Jesus with several passengers. By the time I summoned the courage to visit with him he had to disembark only a few minutes later in Minneapolis. A crowd had gathered around him the entire time that we crossed Wisconsin as if he were the pastor of our railcar's church. He did set the tone of my journey, however, and that was one of seeking.

Following a fitful night's sleep I spent several wondrous hours in the observation car listening to a pair of old farmers pointing out various farm implements *Where's Waldo*-style as we glided through the Great Plains. They both were dressed in bib overalls, as if for the old country variety television show *Hee-Haw*, and acted like they were traveling from Mayberry in the *Andy Griffith Show*. With long unhurried pauses, the conversation went like this:

"Manure spreader."

"Yee-up."

"Combine."

"Uh Huh."

On and on it went with endless implements and machinery

pointed out: bale splitter, big baler, buck rack, mower, harvester, planter, broadcast seeder, cultivator, sprayer, and the full gamut of mechanistic paraphernalia and apparatuses one sees while steaming across North Dakota and Montana. How refreshing it was to eavesdrop on this conversation, as I came to know the plains for the first time from men who lovingly knew it well. These guys were real-deal farmers, and were on the leading edge of a whole host of people I encountered on the train with vastly different backgrounds than what I was familiar with. They were mingled within the traveling ecosystem among people from immense metropolitan areas, businessmen, families, tourists from other countries, and conspicuous Amish families.

The seemingly world-spanning ride across the northern plains was surprisingly interesting and relaxing. With an expectant awareness I paid attention to all the subtleties and details, which provided ample combustible material for this would-be explorer. The train passed along the Missouri River for a spell. Lewis and Clark had paddled here during their epic journey to the Pacific. The waterway flows between lovely hills, and sites of historical significance captivated me. A precious few of these were pointed out, and my imagination more than adequately filled in the remaining details as I scoured the river and horizon for potential areas of interest. A ten-minute stop in Havre (pronounced HAV-er), Montana, provided the first opportunity to stretch my legs outside and enjoy the crisp, cold air. Havre is located at the geographical center of North America. A small monument at the train depot trumpets this fact. It felt significant to this somewhat lonely, aimless, 19-year-old traveling solo.

It was just 10 degrees in the middle of this early November day. The wind whipped across the prairie, "With nothing to stop it but a barb-wired fence, and there wasn't a single barb on it," as Woody Guthrie once uttered. This caused serious trepidation about my first stop at the gateway to Glacier National Park. If it was this cold out on the plains, how frigid would it be in the middle of the night when I was due to disembark way up high in the mountains?

West Glacier is just a flag stop for the train, possessing no depot of any kind. The train only stops if it needs to. With incredible nervousness I strapped on my cumbersome backpack, knowing that it was for real this time. It felt like I was parachuting from a high-flying airplane as I nervously stood at the door of the cozy train looking out at the dark and mysterious world outside, expecting a blast of arctic air as I waited for the hatch to open. I was the only one to exit the safe and cozy train. Remorsefully, I watched as the hundreds of comfortable well-cared-for passengers disappeared into the night as if it was all an elaborate dream. A mild evening of around 30°F greeted me, and this was a profound relief. Seeing the train pull away was unnerving, however. I was left alone in the dark on a small platform.

I visited with some local motel operators who genuinely feared for my safety while warning of bears and a vast web of dangers. Pleading with me as if I was their own child, the couple generously offered a reduced rate of just $30 for the night. They also ushered in reality by informing me that virtually all services in the tiny village of West Glacier were closed during the offseason. Even the visitor center for the national park was shuttered. Since I had forgotten film for my camera, the gentleman offered to help by opening the gas station/restaurant for me in the morning so I could purchase a roll of film and warm up with a cup of coffee. Feeling defeated, and longing for the comforts of predictable life on the train, I opted to camp on village land where I pitched my tent in a patch of snow in order to save money at the beginning of the trip in case it was needed later. I slept spasmodically that first night, often at ten-minute intervals, while repeatedly arising bolt upright in terror after enduring vivid dreams of being mauled by a bear or a pack of wolves.

The temperature plunged below zero while I slept, and it also snowed several inches that night. My hands froze as I took down my tent and forced everything back into my enormous backpack in the wee hours of morning. My toes cried out in protest as they were forced from a warm sleeping bag and stuffed into frozen, inflexible hiking boots. I felt unprepared and shocked by the cold, quickly realizing that nobody would come to the rescue by sucking the feeling back into my toes as my dad had once done.

Everything was shut down in town as if it were boarded up and abandoned prior to the arrival of a hurricane or volcanic explosion. Once again, even the visitor center to this crown jewel of our national park system was closed. I hadn't done any research prior to boarding the train. The difficulties of that first morning stunned me into reality. Luckily I looked barely old enough to be on my own, so strangers were eager to lend a hand. I had overlooked numerous details, such as the seemingly insignificant distance from town to the park, and such matters had to be worked out. Thankfully I was able to hitchhike successfully to the end of the plowed portion of Going-to-the-Sun Road.

On the advice of locals I decided on a place to camp in the backcountry, but it was necessary to contact park headquarters by using the phone at the gas station (technically closed) to obtain the necessary permit and a map. Thankfully the helpful ranger I spoke with was willing to bring these materials out to me, but it took hours for him to make the rendezvous at the trailhead where I waited alone in the cold. Valuable time was lost. When I finally got going I was forced to keep moving in order to have a shot at making it to the area where I wanted to camp prior to nightfall. In retrospect I wish I had paused and reflected on the great beauty that abounded. Lake McDonald was particularly beautiful amidst all the snow and hugged close under the protection of jagged peaks. I assumed there was plenty of time to take it all in later. I'd be heading back that way anyway. Alas, this was not to be the case.

Venturing into the backcountry on foot, I trudged through knee-deep snow. By all accounts, the trail is a nice, wide easy one (the kind that tourists would have mobbed in the summer months), but within an hour and a half it became apparent that I had lost the trail in all the fresh powder. I made a wrong turn somewhere. Instead of a quick three-mile hike to my destination, I ended up on the remarkably scenic and unplowed Going-to-the-Sun Road. Minutes later I had a chance meeting with a cross-country skier heading up the road. If you ever get the chance, this appeared to far and away be the best way to experience Glacier in the winter months. The road is nearly entirely exposed and open to expansive views of the valleys, mountains, alpine glaciers, and breath-taking beauty.

Feeling unsure of myself, it was encouraging to come across another human being out in wilderness that was largely devoid of humanity. The sun was setting, and my resolve to remain in the park had lessened even though I had barely scratched the surface. The alluring girl on skis was of college age and stunning, a real head-turner, and obviously more experienced in wilderness travel, life, and love. Hearing of my wrong turn and story, she scooped me up like a baby bird that had fallen out of its nest, and brought me back to the safety of her house in the nearby town of Whitefish. I spent the next day downhill skiing with Jen and her pot-smoking friends rather than exploring the wilderness that I had travelled 1500 miles to see. While I regretted missing out on so much of Glacier National Park, I was grateful for the neighborliness that may have averted disaster for me.

Numerous locals had implanted real fear into me by telling of hikers who had been mauled over the past couple months due to a poor berry season that had made the bears more ravenous than usual, and also had delayed their hibernation. I was terrified of the creatures with an irrational fear that would have rendered sleeping alone in my tent a highly unpleasant experience. These quick days in Montana were not terribly eventful in terms of wilderness exploration, but they eased me into the rigors of the journey. Future difficulties that otherwise may have seemed insurmountable, I handled calmly and one step at a time. The indispensable assistance of kind strangers continued to come at just the right time.

20

EXPERIENCE OF A LIFETIME

Under cover of darkness, the train lurched through the stunning beauty of the Cascade Mountains in the middle of the night. Securing a seat in the dining car before dawn, the last of the rugged snow-covered peaks were absolutely beguiling at sunrise. I was comfortably snuggled in the dining car among strangers while dining on a princely meal of pancakes and coffee. Though the cakes were served on paper plates, the cost required a king's ransom. It was the only time throughout the entire month that I availed myself of the extravagance, and warm memories of the luxurious experience persist. The small amount of money contained in my wallet needed to last throughout the entire journey, but this one splurge was well worth the expense. As I lingered with a cup of coffee, the horizon gradually widened.

Washington afforded the most varied scenery and extraordinary experiences of the trip. Riding the Empire Builder train to its terminus, I disembarked in Seattle. For

November, and after frigid Montana, the unbelievably balmy temperature in the 50s felt positively tropical. I was awestruck by the verdant greenery of the landscape. Even the grass possessed a far richer and deeper green than the familiar grasses of the Midwest. It was as if I had been deposited into the Promised Land. Leaving the comfort of the train was easy this time, because everyone else was also exiting. Most encouraging was the fact that my new friend Jesse was waiting for me in the station. Never discount the value of hospitality extended to a traveler. It is often the most memorable element of a journey, and something that brings a wayfarer into a blissful state of gratitude. My short stay with him was the highlight of the trip. It was my first opportunity to explore the contours of family life since Andy moved away, as we'll see later.

Among the extended list of generosities was a delightful two-hour drive to Olympic National Park, where a shuttered gate greeted me in a most unwelcoming way. The park had only recently been closed due to a government shutdown caused by a budget battle between President Clinton and the newly elected Republican Congress. Entering the eastern edge of the park, I filled out a card declaring my route across the Olympic Mountain Range and to the western boundary on the other side. This proved to be immensely fortuitous later.

After having spent two days in comfortable accommodations with a loving family, it was difficult to be dropped off by Jesse's affable uncle at a closed, cold, wet park. This was my first real test. It seemed like I was walking into the face of doom. Here there would be no emergency parachute like the beautiful damsel on skis that rescued me when I made a wrong turn in Montana. I felt like crying as my ride drove away and I climbed under the closed gate to walk the unplanned extra miles up the road just to get to the trailhead that would begin my hike on the desired trail. Since this is a major national park incurring over three million visits per year, it was eerie to travel an abandoned road devoid of humanity as if a Chernobyl-like accident had caused the large swath of land to be abandoned. In retrospect the solitude heightened the experience and adventure greatly, but this kid was genuinely scared.

An hour later my fears turned to reality. Climbing Anderson Pass, I was looking forward to spending the night in a three-sided shelter. Steady drizzle was falling. I expected snow on the mountain pass since it was common at the higher elevations in November, even though it is smack dab in the middle of a rain forest. Olympic truly possesses a uniquely diverse ecosystem.

As I steadily climbed higher, I heard a large animal concealed in bushes on a ridge above me. It was relatively low to the ground, although I didn't actually see the creature except for obvious movement of the bushes as it stalked me. I immediately stopped dead in my tracks to peer up at the activity 30 to 40 feet away. My heart pounded in my chest like John Henry's hammer.

The animal likewise froze, and I wishfully hoped that my imagination had conjured up the terror. For good measure I picked up two heavy fist-sized rocks that I carried in both hands for the next 30-odd miles to the other side of the park on the Pacific Ocean side of the Olympic Peninsula.

Proceeding forward, the animal continued to parallel high above me for a full hundred yards. I sang songs, clapped my hands, and yelled up and down the trail to imaginary friends. Thankfully the cat tired of me, but my fear remained. I had been warned of a large population of cougars (aka mountain lions), and that the highest concentration of them in the world was just north of there on Vancouver Island, British Columbia. To this day I'm convinced a large cat was eyeing me up as a potential dinner.

Upon regaining my composure I apprehensively put one foot in front of the other, and finally reached the Anderson Pass shelter. I had a terrible time putting up my fancy new tent due to darkness and frayed nerves. High up on the mountain the damp cold clutched my very soul, so I used the tent for added warmth and the added illusion of safety. Being a 19-year-old on my first big trip by myself, such comforts were indispensable after beginning the journey by being shaken up over the "encounter" with the mountain lion. My inexperience blazed through as I struggled with my easy-to-assemble tent, failed to get my camp stove to work properly to prepare a proper meal, and fumbled with the dead battery in my headlamp (I had no backup, and it was an expensive, hard-to-find specialized variety). Sitting there in the damp chill of the higher elevation at the edge of tree line, it was impossible to imagine safely crossing through the unknown interior of the park where I would surely not see anyone.

Two middle-aged men had previously set up camp in the same shelter, and were having a rough go of it themselves. These more-experienced travelers hadn't ventured far down the valley on the opposite side of the pass, but clearly saw that it was badly flooded and likely impassable. They were abandoning their plans to hike through, and encouraged me to do the same. Another possible emergency exit emerged as they offered to hike out of the park the way we had come in and provide transportation back to civilization. With the troubles I had been having, and the ceaseless cold rain, it just didn't seem that my hike through the beckoning valley (aptly named the "Enchanted Valley") was meant to be. I decided to sleep on it, but was quietly certain of my ultimate decision.

The morning dawned cold and damp. A dense fog packed the area to the point that I didn't even bother hiking through the nearby snowfield to the immediately adjacent, and yet unseen, mountaintop for what would normally be a fantastic panoramic view. While stewing in my abject futility and unpreparedness for the entire trip, a ray of light shined unexpectedly. One of the fellow travelers who eagerly looked to escape the miserable conditions gave me a battery for my headlamp. What a gift! This was like the first caveman being gifted the controlled use of fire, and was enough of a boost to push me over the edge to optimistically continue on through the Enchanted Valley. Wilderness travelers are typically extremely generous, and their kindness toward strangers has often saved lives. This simple act likely salvaged my overall experience of the entire month-long journey, and pulled the trip from the brink of failure.

It was good fortune that I had no concept of the difficulties that lay ahead of me that day. Think of how many of life's greatest experiences would be avoided altogether if we knew of the labyrinth-like logjam of complications in advance. Adventure truly does begin when things go wrong. This single episode is a constant reminder to face life's greatest struggles by putting one foot forward at a time, taking each individual obstacle as it comes, rather than allowing oneself to give in to the inertia that comes from pondering the full weight of all foreseeable problems at once. Though it started inauspiciously, this proved to be one of the most challenging and rewarding days of my life.

I had the entire park to myself for the full glorious stretch to the closed gate at the other side when I hiked out a day and a half later. No friendly strangers appeared out of the ether to help out an inexperienced and poorly prepared kid this time. The coming experience gave me much-needed confidence as I passed through the valley of Hell, and I emerged as a man on the other side.

As I mentioned earlier, the day dawned with a fog so thick that it seemed remarkable that the light drizzle was able to penetrate through the monolith. Being up high on the mountain pass was like being in a cloud. Early on I wondered why I hadn't walked out of the park with such friendly and helpful strangers as they were. Visibility was limited, and I didn't even bother to travel the short one-mile spur trail to Anderson Glacier that otherwise would have been impossible to resist. On clear days the view from that location must present one of the most remarkable, sweeping spectacles on earth. It is a seeming miracle that there are genuine alpine glaciers in such close proximity to honest-to-goodness, bona fide rainforest. I have spent time in a cloud forest and tropical rainforest in Central America, and with a small degree of authority I can tell you that the Olympic Peninsula is the real deal.

The hike through the Enchanted Valley was magical. Alone as I was, with the fog occasionally lifting its skirt to reveal verdant mountains on both sides possessing numerous cataract waterfalls cascading down hundreds of feet all around me, it seemed as if I had ventured into a vast kingdom intended for angels. Never, before or since, have I experienced a more breath-taking or awe-inspiring landscape. Perhaps this was due to the impossible greenness that thrived in mid-November, or the sheer quantity of water that was so overwhelming, or maybe the epic nature of the adventure made the beauty so otherworldly vivid. The endless rain and fog prevented the spectacle from being captured adequately on film, so the images are forever locked in my mind, apparently meant for me alone.

Winter is definitely the rainy season in these parts. "Deluge" season more aptly describes the conditions. I would have thought that discouragement would have weighed heavily upon me due to the omnipresent cold drizzle, but as I gradually became soaked, equilibrium set in. The whole environment was like being submerged in an aquarium with exotic plants.

The trail rapidly descends downward into the valley, beginning high up on the pass near the origin of the Quinault River at the foot of Anderson Glacier near the mountaintop. With dozens and dozens of named and unnamed rivers feeding it from all sides of the valley (bounded to the north, south, and east by mountains), what begins as a typical mountain stream turns into a mighty river within a few short miles. Vast amounts of water flow west in a real hurry. Another name for the Enchanted Valley is the "Valley of

10,000 Waterfalls." While this may be a slight exaggeration, the volume of water being drained from this one valley by this single river defies belief.

The trees, which are positively enormous along much of the route, compete with the clean, fresh water as the main attraction. Some of the largest cedar specimens in the world thrive here, and I encountered a western hemlock with a diameter of over nine feet. Additionally, the Quinault Rainforest holds more of the top-ten known largest Douglas firs than any other area in the world. For reference, only coastal redwood trees reach larger heights than that of the mighty Doug fir. There were many individual standouts, but the overall ancient quality of the forest was most striking. The growing conditions are absolutely ideal, with limitless moisture and temperate weather.

As I followed the Quinault River, my constant companion for the rest of the journey, the trail became increasingly gnarly and difficult to traverse. The Enchanted Valley had become a great basin collecting the dew from heaven. The raging river was a vehicle to disperse this goodness to the rest of the world as it hastened to bequeath its contents into the Pacific Ocean.

Many sections of the trail were entirely washed away by the river, with no visible path across the destruction. Frequently I followed the river as best I could until the trail turned up again, which sometimes involved a half-hour of scrambling along impossibly steep and muddy mountainsides. Early on I took these detours in stride, enjoying the challenge like a newly confident Bilbo Baggins as I forded flooded tributaries while finding my way. I reminded myself that at least there weren't any battles with mosquitoes.

The character of the forest unfolds as you descend inexorably in elevation toward Graves Creek at one of the western entrances to the park, becoming more like popular conceptions of a traditional rainforest. The changes in the forest as you follow the river are fascinating. Moss covers everything in some areas like a thick, sound-muffling quilt, and enormous ferns were as abundant as dandelions. However, the rain became more of an adversary as it fell increasingly harder. It could no longer be classified as a drizzle, and with driving winds, even the marrow in my bones became soaked.

The journey took twice as long as anticipated, and I became discouraged. I was running out of daylight, so I had to pick up the pace. At this time of year the sun is only up for nine hours a day. You can eke out about ten hours if you milk the twilight, and I needed every minute. For a great while it didn't appear that I was going to make it to my destination. After a certain point in the day there was no plan B either, because there were no viable options to set up a bivouac to ride out the night along the trail. Either it was too close to the raging river, or steep mountainside prevented it.

The obstacles became increasingly challenging, and damn near impossible. Many trees were down, and these weren't the kind I was accustomed to that you can just step over (unless you're Paul Bunyan). In one spot a tree was down that thoroughly resembled a skyscraper to my weary body and mind as it descended from the heights, crossing the trail like a monolith as I stared down its mighty trunk into oblivion. It pointed like an arrow shot down from Zeus into the gorge, and blocked my way as if it were the Berlin Wall. It was far thicker in diameter than I am tall. I couldn't climb the wet, craggy bark, so it was necessary to scramble up and around the behemoth.

The only option was to go up the side of the steep, slippery mountain about a hundred feet, and then circumnavigate the massive exposed root system. My heavy pack fully loaded with gear was uncomfortably top-heavy. I slid back down the nearly impassable, muddy incline on my chest to where I started several times. By the time I got around the western hemlock that was likely around 500 years old, I looked like a pipe cleaner that had just cleared a blockage in a sewer pipe. There was no possibility of turning around. I was all in.

Meanwhile the rain pelted relentlessly, and the sun was rapidly disappearing to leave me alone in a wilderness more alive than any I've encountered. With three miles to go, the trail made a dramatic crossing over the raging tempest, which seemed to have become the main artery of the world. From the start of the river up high on that idyllic mountain at the foot of the alpine glacier there are three dozen streams to be counted on the map that serve as tributaries to this point where the trail crosses the river for the last time. However, there are scores more that aren't named on the map. It would be like diagramming every individual capillary of your body! Each of these feeder streams had overflown their banks. Many had to be forded with extreme caution because footbridges had been washed away entirely or submerged. Under normal circumstances these streams may have amounted to little more than trickles allowing the casual hiker to hop from rock to rock. On many of these crossings I was knee or even thigh-deep in water as I stepped precariously over unseen rocks while the former creeks gloried in their newfound statuses as raging torrents. Each of these cascading gushers could have amply powered hydroelectric turbines, because the water was literally plummeting several thousand feet over a short course of one to two miles. Hundreds of cataract waterfalls drop from the steep, rocky cliffs at times of peak flow.

When the clouds weren't socking in the valley completely I was treated to the sight of these magnificent streams on the north, south, and east walls of the valley. The individual rivers would each have been worth an entire day's hike to see their waters race and plummet to the floor of the valley where they merged with the artery that demanded every last drop be squeezed out of the surrounding environment.

The tall, rugged mountains that ring this valley range from 6,000 to well over 7,000 feet above sea level. This may not sound impressive, but keep in mind that sea level in the Pacific Ocean is very close by. The 14,000-foot mountains surrounding the city of Leadville, Colorado, are certainly majestic, but one gazes at them from a street corner within city limits at an elevation over 10,000 feet.

The Enchanted Valley cleaves these mighty peaks, and is less than a mile wide at the start. The first five to seven miles of the hike descend steadily down, down, down, and the valley stays within a width of approximately two miles as the Quinault River cuts through the heart of the valley floor as it drops from 3,000 feet of elevation to 1,700 feet in that span. With tributaries plummeting several thousand feet through such steep topography, the magnificent beauty and deafening roar of the waters frequently induced shock and awe.

This is why the river so quickly develops from humble mountain stream to one of the great rivers of the world (at least when I was there!) over the course of a day's hike. By the time the valley had widened further, and the river itself was at about 800 feet above sea level at my final crossing, there was an extraordinary volume of water flowing fast and deep. Being the only human being inside the entire confines of this magnificent and unforgiving valley heightened the sense of adventure tremendously, but I do wish there was just one other person I could call on the phone occasionally with whom to recollect the shared experience. No doubt the odyssey would have rendered us either best friends or sworn enemies for life.

While passing through in November of 1995 there was an unusual abundance of rainfall, even by Olympic's standards, so the river had become a force to be reckoned with indeed. At one river crossing the bridge possessed only a single railing on the upstream side. The span that hovered over certain doom had become partially dislodged, and tilted uneasily toward the downstream side at a 30- to 45-degree angle. With my cumbersome pack held up by thin chicken legs on a 120-pound frame, I felt like a Weeble. I had no choice but to cross the tempest at this frightening spot. Inch by inch and foot-by-foot I slowly made it over the narrow bridge as wide as a plank while clutching the rail on the high side (praying that it would hold) for all I was worth.

After this moment of great triumph and relief, with the sense that the worst was behind me, I had no time to celebrate. Over three miles of travel during dusk and twilight hours awaited me, so I employed a walk/run truffle shuffle in desperation before the light of the world was extinguished. A mile before reaching the abandoned campground I encountered the most stubborn and insurmountable obstacle yet.

21

TALKING TO THE ANIMALS

Suddenly, and as unexpectedly as stumbling across a unicorn, I found myself smack dab in the middle of a huge herd of elk blocking the trail. This major roadblock felt like an ambush of sorts. I knew nothing about the animal, and was dismayed to discover that such a large creature would huddle up in a gang like this. About 30 of them were lined up above me to my left on a ridge, and several more were encamped on the trail itself that was cut into the steep mountainside. These were Roosevelt elk, the largest variety in North America, and bulls can tip the scales at nearly 1,000 pounds. I implored them to leave, but they weren't the least bit afraid of me. All eyes of the beasts were fixated on me as if I was the evening's entertainment.

It was raining much harder now, becoming alarmingly dark, and I was completely exhausted. The large rack of antlers prominently displayed above the fireplace at Cascade Restaurant was the extent of my limited knowledge of the animal. I was more familiar with the moose of Minnesota, which are a more solitary creature. When one comes across a bull moose it is best to view them from a safe distance. This is especially the case during mating season in the fall when they are in rut. A couple months earlier someone in a compact car on the Gunflint Trail in northern Minnesota had pulled over to view a bull moose along the side of the road. The bright beams of light enraged the giant beast, and it promptly rammed the vehicle at full speed. The car crumpled like a discarded beer can and was thrown into the ditch, totaled. A bull moose is a force to be reckoned with, standing over six feet tall at the shoulder, along with a well-endowed rack of antlers spanning four to six feet. They are formidable creatures to be respected from a distance.

Elk aren't quite as large as moose, but they are the next largest in the deer family. A bull elk with a full rack of antlers is a stunning well-apportioned creature with an intimidating and regal presence befitting a king. Here I stood in their presence as a helpless waif, utterly beseeching their mercy. My only other experience with elk had come in Rocky Mountain National Park a month earlier in Colorado.

I was camping with two best friends: Andy, whom we met out there for an extended weekend, and my buddy Dan. Due to frigid, snowy conditions and below-zero wind chills, it became necessary for us to illegally make camp in a scrubby thicket of trees. We huddled around a smoky fire at 11,040 feet of elevation, practically inches below tree line, in a small valley dominated by peaks rising straight up in protection of beautiful Timber Lake. We were exhausted from the exertions of the day while gloomily eating raw cakes of

Ramen Noodles, because I hadn't brought the proper fuel for my camp stove. (It turns out that a 99-cent bottle of rubbing alcohol obtained from the pharmacy fails to sustain a flame for more than about ten seconds. Who knew?) A sense of foreboding loomed due to unpredictable weather conditions that could markedly deteriorate at any time. From somewhere within the fog that mysteriously enshrouded the landscape, the most unusual, unearthly, primal sound I had ever heard repeatedly reverberated off the mountains in the cold, snowy backcountry. We were the only humans within miles of our camp. The loud, spooky, inharmonious, mournful-sounding cacophony made my blood curdle in fright. Turning to my Coloradan friend without a hint of irony, I asked if it was a Sasquatch. Chuckling at the ignorance of a flatlander, Andy said it was just a bull elk bugling. It was likely in rut (aka uncontrollably horny) and best to be avoided.

This conveys a bit of the terror I felt to be in close proximity to not just one of the monsters, but dozens. My situation felt hopeless, and this literally felt like the kiss of death. No amount of will power would get me through to safety as I stood out there alone in driving rain so far away from anyone else. For lack of ideas, the only thing I could think of was to sing songs and speak gently to them.

My audience listened politely, and didn't interrupt in the least. Their curiosity was piqued over the mannerisms of this strange creature performing for them in the twilight. It seemed as if I might have to bed down with them for the night, but the mountainside was impossibly steep at this point. Additionally, the winds were at gale force and I feared camping near any tall trees.

The elk simply were not going to leave. I was especially
fearful of the bulls with their large racks of antlers containing
points more than capable of skewering me. They eyed me
carefully with an obvious lack of trust. I finally got the nerve
to walk between the bulls, about 15 feet above me, and the
numerous females to my immediate right. I was certain this
was ill-advised under any circumstances, but I was desperate.
One cow blocking the trail took her sweet time getting out of
my way. As I very slowly walked by she turned toward me
and I could see that she was huge! The dignified female
looked straight into me with intelligent eyes as she called out
to her friends in a tone reminiscent of a cross between a
Holstein cow and a goat. What a magnificent creature. I
cautiously passed within five feet of her as my heart pounded
in fear while expecting to imminently be charged and gored
by the bulls that were definitely on high alert.

While I was mesmerized by this slow process of shuffling
down the trail at a snail's pace past this one elk, I casually
looked down the mountainside to my right to discover at least
20 more elk. This herd comprised no less than 50 individuals.
It was incredible. With my limited knowledge I carefully
passed between the formidable array of bull elks that were
lined up in a strong battle position above the harem of cows
they had apparently collected below. I prayed for safety as I
had never prayed before, and though I had lost 45 valuable
minutes due to the delay, I was profoundly grateful to have
emerged unscathed. There was no time for celebration or
rest, however. I still was not out of the woods. Glancing over
my shoulder to catch one last glimpse of my new friends that

were seemingly oblivious to the powerful storm, I trudged onward as a changed man in the company of my maker, who seemed to be providing special protection.

22

NEARLY SWEPT AWAY BY A MONSOON

Complete and utter darkness sealed me off from any
semblance of safety. The rain poured down in sheets
horizontally as the wind gained strength. I was exhausted to
the point of being nearly broken down both mentally and
physically. At long last I arrived at the Graves Creek
Campground without breathing my last breath, but I still
worried about the possibility. It had become very cold at
around 38°F, and the sky opened up in an absolutely
monsoonal deluge with extremely high winds. It felt like I was
putting my tent up underwater. The environment had
become more aquatic than terrestrial. The sound of the
driving rain and high winds blotted out everything else,
causing me to focus on nothing but survival. From all
directions I could hear the sound of mighty trees, which had
withstood centuries of such abuse, crashing down from the
gale-force winds.

In a flurry I threw my tent together, dumping everything

including myself inside. As the rain intensified, continuing to pound harder and harder, I hurriedly unrolled my sleeping bag. I was very cold at this point. I shivered uncontrollably, sensed a slow mental response, and could hardly enable my hands (which had spent the day exposed to the elements) to respond to commands. Hypothermia was settling in and advancing.

Suddenly I found myself, including the sleeping bag upon which I knew I depended for survival, sitting in a full inch of water inside my tent. In an absolute rage, because I had paid good money for this tent, I stormed outside to dismayingly discover that in a span of just five minutes a small lake had formed around the tent. I could see nothing in the pitch-black darkness. The driving rain from the typhoon pierced to my bones, but somehow I summoned the strength to drag the tent with everything in it onto a higher area that was essentially a large rock.

Diving into the tent I stripped off all my soaked clothing, and submerged myself into the synthetic North Face sleeping bag. To my amazement, the big bulky thing that cost me $200 was completely dry even after having soaked in water. It would have been worth my life's savings that night. I am convinced I would have died without it.

Swaddled in luxury and slowly warming up, I managed to scrawl out the following in big letters in my journal:

I AM MISERABLE.
Everything is wet.
Pouring outside. I guess
I am in the rainforest!
<u>Please help me God.</u>

I had walked, scratched, shuffled, clawed, climbed, and eked out 20 hellacious miles that day. My body and bones felt every bit of it.

The one who is Lord even over the elements didn't abandon me. Eventually my body temperature rose to the level of toastiness, and I enjoyed a remarkably comfortable night. Outside the confines of my small tent the storm raged on with a ferocity that verged on the horrific. Immense trees continued to crash to the forest floor from lofty heights of 200 to 300 feet, possessing circumferences greater than 20 feet. Sometimes I felt the tremendous thud through the ground beneath me. They had proudly stood as sentinels over their dominion since the Renaissance, the discovery of the New World, and the Reformation.

My immediate area was relatively safe with younger trees, however, and it was quite peaceful inside. The contrast was striking with the only thing separating my cozy well-lit bubble of peace from death and mayhem being the thin nylon walls of my high-end tent that flailed wildly as if in a hurricane, appearing to near the point of collapse at times. Once again, this was an item worth splurging on. It flexed and billowed in and out violently with the howling blasts of wind. Thankfully it held fast. Would I have survived in something of lesser quality? I doubt it.

Gradually I settled in as if I was cuddled up next to a fireplace, and finished reading *The Call of the Wild* by Jack London. I will never forget the experience. There is nothing quite like feeling absolutely safe in a refuge while the worst kind of storm unleashes its wrath immediately outside. By 7:30 p.m. I sailed away into the coma-like sleep of a bear in the winter.

This part of the rainforest, on the western side of the mountains, receives anywhere from 12 to 14 feet of rain per year. Yes, that's feet. The mountains jut out from the sea into the clouds, and consequently wring the moisture out of storms as they rise above the Olympic Mountains. Thus the western slopes and valleys receive epic amounts of rain. The eastern slope lies in the rain shadow, receiving a comparatively scant total of about 25 inches of rain per year. What a remarkable contrast in a park and state full of variety. A mere mile can separate seemingly wholly different worlds.

The mountains themselves receive enormous amounts of snow. Mount Olympus, being the highest peak in the park at 7,980 feet, can receive 50 to 70 feet of snow per year. This massive snowfall supports approximately 266 active glaciers in the national park. It is positively surreal to have a genuine alpine environment in such close proximity to a flourishing temperate rainforest. It's a true wonder of the world.

23

THIRST. MADNESS. RESCUE

Following a wild night in the tent with the storm raging outside, I emerged in the morning from the safety of my cocoon as if I had survived the Battle of the Bulge. The winds and rain had ceased. Overcast skies placidly illuminated the wreckage wrought from the upheaving disturbance that seemed to have turned the world upside down and shook it violently. The serenity was somewhat akin to what hurricane survivors may experience after climbing out of a bunker the morning after.

Though I only possessed a few swallows of water, a mere four ounces, I was too lazy to boil water for drinking. What an infuriating hassle this can be on a morning when all you want to do is pack up and head out. There's the unpacking of the stove, filling it with fuel, boiling the water, allowing it to cool, and on and on. I hadn't thought of bringing a water filter, so I was forced to endure this ridiculous process.

I managed to avoid using the stove throughout the duration of this journey, other than the five minutes of failing to make it work at Anderson Pass. I merely subsisted on the occasional granola bar, having consumed just three of them the day before. At times one may skimp on food, but running out of water is never advisable. I planned on a quick six-mile hike to the cross bar at the edge of the national park, and then hoped to hitch a ride to the nearest town. Unfortunately things didn't work out so smoothly.

I trudged along on a death march, even though the way was fairly flat and easy-going. My pack weighed a ton from all the wet gear and clothing inside. Later in the day I weighed the pack since it felt so outrageously heavy. The bastard was 10% heavier than when I started due to all the extra moisture in everything. My shoulders and hips screamed for mercy, but like a greedy taskmaster I granted them none. I ached all over like Indiana Jones after having been dragged under a truck in *Raiders of the Lost Ark*, who when pressed by his beautiful admirer seeking one undamaged spot that might be kissed in gratitude, annoyingly pointed to his elbow. Additionally, bothersome blisters bedeviled my shoulders, feet, and hips.

It is an odd thing to feel overwhelming thirst when your clothes are wet, everything being carried is waterlogged to the point of sloshing around, and just 20 feet to your right is a river running at flood stage. I was just certain that a car would pass by to rescue me shortly after I got to the main road.

Reality became a cruel friend as I plodded ten miles that day on virtually no water, food, or even spiritual nourishment. The complete lack of traffic was thoroughly frustrating. The map made this road seem reasonably important. I had hiked across Olympic National Park in two days, which is far too fast, and it was terribly taxing due to the conditions. With all the flooding I just didn't think I had much choice. I would definitely advise a more leisurely pace when you make this journey. By most accounts it is not generally a very difficult trek.

Parts of the South Shore Road that I lumbered and waddled endlessly along after leaving the park looked like a bona fide war zone. I begrudgingly hoisted myself over many very large downed trees as it followed the Quinault River on its increasingly anxious quest to reach the Pacific Ocean. At a point of desperation, while battling exhaustion and enjoying a herd of elk bounding through the forest, I turned my head back to the road and was stunned to find that 200 yards of it had been completely washed away. There was a clean break punctuated by a six-foot drop to muddy water, muck, and churning chaos below. The relentless onslaught of high rushing water had eroded it from below until it collapsed into an impassable witch's brew of pavement, mud, and an incredible tangle of trees and flood debris. This was just one more obstacle among many previously handled with relative dexterity, but without the excitement of experiencing more of the park, it was horribly demoralizing and seemed hopelessly impassable.

After passing wide around it, climbing over more detritus and mud, I expended the last of my energy reserves and finally got through it. Then, after not seeing a soul since leaving the mountain high above the valley, I came across a law enforcement ranger right there on civilization's side of the wreckage as I tossed my backpack onto the asphalt atop the last precipice. He was assessing the damage, and I was absolutely elated to see him. I felt like I had scaled Everest with my last dying wisp of energy, and had inexplicably found a tourist tram at the top that would quickly and safely bring me back down. I was weary beyond the point of exhaustion, begrimed head-to-toe with bits and pieces from every long mile of the Enchanted Valley, and must have had a trace of madness in my eyes when we made eye contact.

Even though the federal government was shut down and the park was closed, workers considered essential were kept in employment for situations like this. Somebody had checked the permit box on the other side of the mountains, and told him I was coming. Due to the violence of the storm and severe flooding, they thought I might not have been able to make it across the park, and were beginning the process of searching for me from both ends. The ranger was so very friendly. I latched on to him like he was long lost family. It reminds me of the young kindergarten boy who caught my eye after disembarking from a school bus to an elementary school where I was substitute-teaching years later. He held on to my hand for dear life while exclaiming, "You're my daddy!"

The knight in shining armor deposited me in the tiny village of Quinault, a hamlet of refuge and beguiling charm. I would have succumbed to insanity, thirst, and exhaustion without him. Once again a stranger had stepped in to rescue me from disaster at the very moment of greatest necessity.

24

BLESSED. BAKED. BUSED.

The record seemed to skip as I stepped across the threshold
of a diner crowded with locals. My disheveled, waterlogged,
and filthy appearance, combined with the larger-than-life
backpack, made it impossible to blend in. I stood frozen in
place for a moment as I became unexpectedly shocked to re-
enter the presence of humankind.

Almost immediately a friendly stranger, Walt, confidently
addressed me on behalf of the onlookers by saying, "You look
like you could use a good meal." Indeed I could, having
subsisted on only a few granola bars over the past couple
days, and being as miserably dehydrated as I was.

This saint of a Good Samaritan, a paragon of virtue,
proceeded to buy me the best hamburger and fries of my life
along with a hot chocolate, and sat with me as I regaled him
with tales of the trip. I can handle long periods alone in the
wilderness or in the cozy confines of a room, but flying solo in

a crowded public place while transitioning from solitude can bring me to my knees in loneliness. Walt provided the perfect realigning portal back into society. Meeting kindly people like him was among the highlights of my month-long pilgrimage.

Upon receiving life-sustaining nourishment, I perked right up like a neglected plant finally given water. After the meal I was treated to a close up view of the world's largest Sitka spruce tree, which grows right in town and boasts an astonishing 18-foot diameter at its base. I left with a prized cone as a souvenir, which I promptly lost.

All I'm left with from this experience are memories. As mentioned previously, the ever-present rain and dark skies ruined the pictures. Even with bouts of depression and despair, this had been the most memorable and satisfying coming-of-age adventure of my life. I had passed through the valley of the shadow of death and emerged a man. My young faith in God had also strengthened into an unbreakable bond during the ordeal. He had become my steady companion through thick and thin.

The journey from Quinault to the next town that had Greyhound bus service required hitchhiking. The very first vehicle to come along pulled over. The willingness of generous strangers to assist almost defies belief. It was a large, old pickup truck. The bench seat seemed to be eight feet long as it comfortably housed the driver (a burly no-nonsense fellow who was perhaps a logger), and each of his four quiet young children lined up along with yours truly. The feller clearly didn't take kindly to all the tree-hugging interlopers that must invade his country during the tourist season in droves as fanny-pack-clad locusts. Still, he picked me up with little thought apparently given to it, and with even fewer words.

In the next town I waited for my bus in a coffee shop while treating myself by carbo-loading with a fluffy baked potato fit for a king. I wrote home about it as a spellbound suitor might pine over a lover or a mythical mountain. The entire trip was punctuated by long hours of waiting due to not having a vehicle and frequently having many hours to kill. One of the valuable lifelong lessons gained was the art of successful, enjoyable waiting, so as not to allow the time to disappear as a waste. I always had a book at the ready, pen and journal, or a postcard to write to distant friends.

Everywhere I went my backpack and I drew curious onlookers as if we were a ventriloquist and dummy. People enjoyed hearing where I had been and where I was going almost as much as I enjoyed telling it. Eventually it was time to catch the bus, and I was shocked to discover that it would only cost 25 cents to travel over 40 miles. Afterward a free transfer ticket carried me another 50 miles to Olympia, the capitol.

The journey seemed to drag on relentlessly until I finally arrived in the bustling city well after dark at a well-lit outdoor bus terminal in a rough part of town. I was greeted by the unsettling knowledge that the next bus to Seattle wouldn't depart until early the next morning. Standing there alone under the lights, after having been steadily moving forward in the wilderness, was frightening. I called the family I had been staying with, perhaps 90 minutes away, begging for a ride.

The hospitality they showed me, a passing wayfarer, was nothing short of extraordinary. My only association with them was that of being a roommate of one of their relatives in a cabin in distant Minnesota.

Amazingly, one of them rescued me from my plight by swooping in to deliver me back to their home in the middle of the night, where I promptly fell into a heap after one of the longest days of my life. My only regret is that I had nobody to share these outrageous memories with, until you passed along with me just now.

25

PEOPLE MATTER

Meaningful connections with people are indispensable to our well-being. The full week spent in Washington helped me see and feel this vividly, while it also affirmed the value of temporary solitude. We are designed to be in community, to know and be known, love and be loved, while laughing and sharing in the joys and trials of life with others.

My solo trek across Olympic National Park was so epic in nature that I'll likely never experience anything like it for the rest of my life. The highlight of my entire month circumnavigating the west and exploring the boundaries of my life, however, was lodging with and enjoying a loving and generous family in Bremerton, Washington, for several days. Through short excursions, they introduced me to the wonders of the area. Sharing meals together around the large table provided some of the most meaningful experiences. This was the first stable family I had achieved such familiarity with since Andy moved away two and a half years earlier.

I wasn't just some stranger crashing on the couch. Rather, I was admitted into the inner circle of their tribe during my stay. I am forever grateful for the experience, which unbeknownst to them was a formative chapter in my life.

My access into their home was through my roommate Eric, in northern Minnesota. Like an anthropologist, I studied the details of his family with fascination. They seemed to be entirely of another species. For one thing, they dwarfed the rest of humanity. Eric's parents and one of his brothers, who was then a professional basketball player in Europe, spent a weekend over Christmas with us at the cabin. I felt fortunate to celebrate the holiday with them. Both his dad and brother stand just a half-inch below seven feet tall. This required them to duck significantly, as if bowing, whenever crossing the threshold. I was a pygmy among giants.

They were an intact, close-knit family, which was foreign and exotic to me. Additionally, they all spoke openly about their faith. Eric's brothers were clean-cut, permanently situated with beautiful wives, and were well established in respectable professions. Eric, on the other hand, looked like a scraggly gold miner hopelessly eking out a living in the Yukon subsisting on hard tack.

Back in his college days he had been a highly desirable fetch for the ladies as a 6-foot 8-inch basketball star at Bethel College. Even though he was handsome, successful as a student, and with girls, his ambition after graduation was simply to live in a shack as deeply in the woods as possible while only earning a subsistence-level income. Though his college degree from the private college had certainly cost in the neighborhood of $100,000, he had transformed himself into a reclusive, burly, lumberjack-looking sort of fellow while working at the local lumber mill. His parents must have been concerned, but I never observed the slightest hint of it. A rare unconditional love was their chief identifying characteristic, as distinct and noticeable as gender or race.

It was with their extended family that I had taken up quarters in Washington. This nuclear family was likewise loving and caring. They were settled in a beautiful home overlooking the Puget Sound where you could see across the water to Seattle and beyond to the Cascade Mountains on clear days. Their clean-cut, good-looking children were also on a bright path of undoubted success. I found it fascinating that everyone in this family going back a couple generations, as well as Eric's, had attended the same Christian College, Bethel, in Minnesota, even though the families hailed from the far-flung states of Washington and Ohio. Once again, bright futures, all.

Then along came the black sheep, Jesse. He was 17 years old, had long hair paired with a scruffy mustache, and was poised to drop out of high school. He was a good kid that was mature beyond his years, and was very kind to me. Something in him rebelled against the accepted way of doing things. All things being equal, and kids being raised similarly within the confines of an adoring family, what causes this? He was to become the first offspring of the extended family to not ultimately attend Bethel, and eschewed the notion of college altogether. Everyone worried about Jesse, knew he was smart, and lamented that he didn't seem to apply himself.

Interestingly enough, at least to this writer who formerly

dreamed of being a garbage man as a child and still fancies the idea, years later he bought an old garbage truck with a buddy and started his own waste hauling business. He undercut the competition with cheaper rates due to having no employees and very little overhead. Who does this? He was determined to go his own way. Certainly he exceeded his own expectations, as he ultimately acquired a small fleet of garbage trucks in building a business of significant size.

Jesse didn't rebel against anyone in particular. He had no animosity for his family that I could see, and they loved him unconditionally. He rebelled against a system—the conventional career path—and needed to be beholden to no man or the expectation of others. I have enormous respect for how he found his own way. Might he now feel somewhat shackled by his success in business, and the constraints and busyness that inevitably must come with it? I wouldn't know. Though I was adopted as a family member during my stay and would seemingly remain a lifelong friend, we never kept in touch after I left. Proximity is crucial to virtually every relationship.

I have always had the same dissatisfaction with the status quo. Thus far I have not been able to parlay this into any kind of "success" in terms of a career. For 12 years I found myself working lower-level jobs laboring for "The Man" in the bowels of Corporate America. This was the one thing I always wanted to avoid. I look up to those intrepid entrepreneurs who find another way. Now, due to a recent layoff that has prompted the writing of this book, I have been released from my slavery to the system. Having a family and a mortgage to feed and care for certainly complicates matters, but I have been gifted with a second chance to forge my own path. Perhaps this will be another story someday.

As a 19-year-old my unending discontent and lamentation over the conventional and fashionable life-track kept my mind in a constant state of turbulence like the Quinault River, as it churned over my unguided emotions and raging impulses. Enjoying extended quality time with a loving family was most soothing to my soul. Both the quality and extended aspects have always been key, and this is remarkably rare. Otherwise I felt like a homeless man gawking through the window at the patrons of a five-star restaurant, unable to connect and be satisfied. This family almost certainly has no concept of the level of impact they had on me. My relationship with them, short as it was, is cherished in my very soul.

Not many months prior to this, any chance encounters with other families and observations of the normal friendships they enjoyed caused me to feel utterly alone in the world. It was for this reason that I became so addicted to television as a child, and hoarded dozens of pets in my room. All this was behind me now. I was a clean slate absorbing information while grasping hold of positive influences like this family to steer me toward the well-lived life. Additionally, I felt comfortable in my own skin. I was no longer engulfed by an all-consuming tsunami-like wave of inferiority when in the presence of people who had their acts together.

These new friends freely gave of their time and resources as they shared many of their favorite places with me. We explored the city of Seattle. Mountain climbing on the Olympic Peninsula and astride the Cascade Mountain range far to the east in their company was a delight.

One hike up a 7,000-foot peak was particularly memorable. Standing on top of the mountain, we were so close to Mt. Rainier that it seemed as if I could scrape the snow off the imposing volcano. The weather was a remarkable contrast to what I had endured in Olympic National Park, being delightfully sunny and in the mid-60s. From atop this peak I could see all the major volcanoes in the region, including Mt. Baker, Rainier, Mt. St. Helens, and others. This was a rare luminous November day allowing a full view to the north and south Cascades, and the Olympic Range clear across the Puget Sound to the west. There was so very much to be thankful for.

I was particularly enamored by Mount Rainier. Larger than life, it looms imposingly at 14,410 feet right from sea level. It towers one and a half miles in height above the neighboring peaks, and seems completely out of place in its neighborhood. This active volcano absolutely dominates and owns the landscape on a clear day.

The day I left to catch the train that would whisk me out of the state, I boarded the ferry in Bremerton before sunrise for the relaxing ride to Seattle. The rising sun lit the sky with brilliant shades of red and orange. The reflection off snow-capped Rainier set the mountain afire in glorious beauty and color. I was utterly amazed. The extraordinary display had a palliative effect that relieved some of the sadness brought on from heading onward by myself.

26

COMING DOWN FROM THE MOUNTAINTOP

A cloud of depression awaited me in Portland. I walked a short distance to the Greyhound bus station, and discovered in dismay that the bus I wanted to ride to the Columbia River gorge wasn't leaving until very late in the day. These are the sorts of problems I hadn't thought of when planning for the trip by simply staring at a large map of the United States. I couldn't bear the thought of wandering around the big city with my heavy backpack all day, so I asked a random stranger where I should go to experience the famous Oregon coast. I was thinking of the beautiful rugged coastline seen in the movie *The Goonies,* but didn't mention that specifically. He said I should go to Lincoln City. "It's beautiful there."

After buying my bus ticket I had several hours to kill, and spent it walking aimlessly around the city of Portland afraid to spend any money. I had brought along just $200 for the entire trip, and it needed to last for the duration. At one point a ragged-looking black man approached me. Afraid of appearing prejudiced, I engaged him in conversation. He was quite friendly. Eventually he looked me straight in the eye to add gravity to what he was saying, and asked me point blank, "Are you cool?" Not understanding, I hesitantly replied, "Yeah….. I'm cool," knowing damn well that I was definitely not "cool." He leaned in closer and more gravely this time, "No, are you cool." With the high voice of a little kid I answered in the affirmative again, "Yeah, I'm cool." We went back and forth in this manner four or five times until he finally opened his trench coat.

My eyes widened to discover a large quantity of drugs hanging on small hooks of seemingly every shape, shade, style, variety, and method of consumption. The entire lining of his coat was impressively festooned with hallucinogens, much like an avid fly fisherman might use every available space of real estate on his hat to hold hand-tied flies.

Quickly I confessed, "No, I'm not cool." Hesitating to let me go, like some big fish, he turned to his side business as a pimp. I must have had a look of despair about me. Eventually I freed myself from his grasp, only to be turned loose to wander in the loneliest of places, the middle of a large city. After walking aimlessly for a time, I turned into a Christian Science reading room.

The elderly woman watching the empty place was engaging and very interested in me. Pouring out my heart, I shared some spiritual struggles. In response she passionately shared her love for the writings of Mary Baker Eddy, the founder of her faith. She was convinced that I had to have a copy of her foundational book, *Christian Healing*. Since I couldn't afford the $21.95 price tag, she exacted a promise to read the whole thing in lieu of payment. Touched by the offer, I readily agreed. Ultimately I had to break the promise after making it partway through on the train. It was readily apparent that Christian Science was nothing more than a well-organized cult, a shadow of the real thing.

After four-and-a-half hours of an unplanned zombie-like walk as a vagrant in the city, I spent the next four hours sitting at a table in the bus station. Time seemed to move in reverse as I glanced at the clock every ten minutes. An hour passed with me sleeping face down in a pool of drool. Another hour ended with a sore wrist as I chronicled the gaps that remained in my journal from the week in Washington, where I wished I could return. With great relief I finally boarded the bus bound for Lincoln City. Though it was just 90 miles away, the ride took three hours and capped off an incredibly long and boring day. Train travel is far more fulfilling than riding the bus!

27

A BRIAR PATCH GROWS IN LONELY COUNTY

Lincoln City was the pits. I was stunned to discover that it was the sort of tourist town I normally strive to avoid. Even worse, it was heralded as offering the only extended stretch of sandy beach (seven miles) in the Pacific Northwest. I had come to experience the rugged coast, which was apparently plentiful everywhere else! The entire length of the beach was lined with hotels, restaurants, and a plethora of tourist establishments that were nearly all closed for the season.

What a disaster! I was stuck there for three days. Aghast by my misfortune and poor planning, I found a spot on the beach behind a log a little after midnight and went to sleep. The next morning I bit the bullet after waking up in a drizzle, and parted with $62 for a two-night stay in a mostly empty hotel for a room that had an ocean view.

Self-consciously I settled my weary burned-out body and mind into the hot tub, trying to ignore the orders of a sign remarking that nobody under age 21 was allowed unsupervised.

Returning to my room I glanced at the phone book, and the letters very clearly spelled out Lonely County. Blinking in disbelief, they reassembled themselves before my eyes as Lincoln County. The mind can certainly do strange things, even without the influence of drugs.

Once again I was a little fish in what felt like a great big town. I searched the yellow pages under clergy, and dialed Pastor Carl Reynolds at random. I asked if he'd bestow a bit of his knowledge on me, and amazingly he met me in the hotel restaurant to pay me a visit. After a stimulating conversation about faith and life, the older gentleman paid for my breakfast. That evening I went to a service at his church, and enjoyed singing hymns with the 70 or so congregants. This connection with the relatively dry, but well-meaning, pastor would prove to be providentially serendipitous.

Bolstered by friendship, inoculated against the nagging loneliness, I spent the next day walking 15 miles round trip on the beach so I could catch the tiniest glimpse of that famed, roughhewn, irregular, jagged Oregon coast I so wanted to experience. The mere mile walked among these surroundings far away from the characterless establishments of Lincoln City was very beautiful to this Midwesterner, and worth the effort of escaping the beaten path. On a secluded beach I thrilled in seeing 50 to 60 sea lions, starfish, anemones, and other creatures that were completely unknown and exotic to me. This was so much more interesting and satisfying than sand, hotels, and restaurants!

The main excitement in Oregon occurred during the wee hours of Thanksgiving Day. I woke up bolt upright in terror at 4:00 a.m., fearful of missing my bus that was due to pick me up at a location a mile away. As was customary, I found a way to end up running late. After ten minutes of a nerve-wracking gallop down dark, unfamiliar city streets while saddled with my backpack, I found the parking lot of the small casino where I was to board the bus. Eureka. I made it! Unfortunately, the road I was skipping down dead-ended a block prior to my destination. Like a mouse, I frantically ran back and forth looking for a magic passageway through the maze to the cheese. According to the clock I did not have time to run several blocks all the way around via the major streets.

Eventually I found an empty lot that led directly to the bus stop. In the darkness it appeared that after I bruised through some large bushes I would be home free in tall grass. Such an assessment was akin to Canada ordering a full-scale invasion of the United States based on the appearance of an undefended border. Little did I know that I was all in for an epic battle with nature.

The bus stop was fortified in the rear (my direct path) with blackberry bushes and briars that pierced the skin like barbed wire. These weren't the cute little blackberry bushes we have in the Midwest that possess a sort of prickly fuzz in comparison. No, this briar patch would have tried the patience of the one and only Brer Rabbit. Making things even more interesting was the presence of actual barbed wire seemingly placed at random throughout the empty lot, as if I was traveling through a World-War-I-era no man's land.

Never have I seen an area so thick with thorny bushes. They must have all been gathered there for a national convention for the express purpose of keeping me off that bus. Frankly, I'm surprised I even made it out. I could be a pack of bones in that lot right now, some 20 years later, and nobody would be the wiser. My hands burned in extreme pain from the onslaught of cuts and unwelcome blood draws. Being in a hurry only made things worse. Bushes seemed to grab me from behind and throw me to the ground in their attempt to squeeze the life out of me.

In an absolute panic I tried rushing through like a bull in a china shop, but that mired me in the tangles even more. My colossal pack made traveling through the hellhole nearly impossible. I fell down dozens of times into the mud, and just wanted to stay down there crying. My heart pumped at maximum capacity, and the anxiety level was redlining.

It took me 15 minutes to bruise and cut through 100 feet of terrain apparently designed to keep devils out. When I finally made it through it was as if I had completed a marathon. I was completely relieved to see the bus idling there waiting for me! With a fresh influx of adrenaline all the pain left my body as I ran toward the motor coach in all-out desperation. When I was within ten feet of the rear of the bus, like a mirage, the damn thing drove away. I still think the bastard behind the wheel saw me in the well-lit parking lot. The visage of my frightening appearance charging toward the bus with my last ounce of energy must have scared him off. I yelled, screamed, and jumped up and down to no avail.

Adrenaline departing as suddenly as it had come, my hands

instantly swelled in pain like nobody's business. I was also covered from head to toe in mud and blood. My entire body had sustained cuts, and my nylon camping pants were torn badly. Many of the thorns remained embedded in my body for several days. My hands continued to burn, as if from a severe sunburn, for some time. I looked like death warmed over. I am positive that I'm the first person stupid enough to have crossed through that briar patch. That is my claim to fame.

Stumbling into a quickee mart, I had the audacity to call Pastor Reynolds at 6:15 in the morning. Waking the poor guy up, all I could think of saying was, "I'm sorry. Did I wake you up?"

This was Thanksgiving Day, and the son of a gun picked me up, no questions asked, to drive me back to the hotel. Unbelievable. The hotel staff let me back into my room to clean up, because I was literally a bloody mess. The Oregon mud became an enduring souvenir on my clothes, often serving as a prop for future stories told about the ordeal, after I attempted washing my clothes in the washer.

After this desperate plight fit for the ages, Pastor Carl Reynolds redeemed it all by inviting me to Thanksgiving dinner. A few hours later he and his wife picked me up at the hotel, and together we dashed off for the high country in their car. We were destined to meet my train south of Portland in Salem, and had ample time to partake in Thanksgiving dinner at the International House of Pancakes. How great is that? I devoured the food as if I were a newly rescued prisoner of war. The meal was so good that it ranks up there among the most enjoyable Thanksgiving dinners of my life. I was grateful not only for the lift, but to not have to spend the holiday alone. The saint of a man even treated me to the meal. He and his wife then got me to the train station with time to spare. I hope their children will someday read this account of my gratitude.

As if that wasn't enough, at the very spot near the train platform where I was left, a young couple (George and Jenny) treated me to a beer as we waited together. Thanksgiving Day, which had begun so inauspiciously, had become one of my favorite all-time holiday experiences due to these encounters with kindness. For some reason the mere sight of me prompted complete strangers to engage in cheerful charity, which is the only kind blessed by God. Next time you bless a traveler with some small act of kindness, you might be touching their heart to such a degree that their entire day or journey is salvaged.

28

JOY IN THE JOURNEY

Riding the rails is a feast along a bountiful reservoir of time. It is not the dull life of an heiress in *Downton Abbey*. I learned the art of remarkably restful and productive leisure while savoring books, writing letters, reminiscing, journaling, watching the countryside drift by, and visiting with interesting people who were in no particular hurry. Dozing off whenever the urge struck, sleepy eyes casually opened hours later to reveal entirely new environments, landscapes, and habitats. In retrospect, I can see my ideal concept of leisure was shaped by these remarkable days and hours of refreshment.

A well-deserved nap had carried me across the border into sunny California. Warmer temperatures welcomed me in the city of Merced in a manner akin to hula girls greeting travelers arriving on the tarmac in Hawaii. The sunshine was extravagantly luxurious following a prolonged stay in the Pacific Northwest.

I had a full hour to stretch my legs prior to catching a bus bound for Yosemite National Park, which cost me nothing since I came in on the Amtrak. Venturing into a farmers' market, my eyes widened to discover a cornucopia filled with fresh fruits and vegetables. With change rattling around in my pockets, I bought the largest bunch of bananas I had ever seen. Though they obviously weren't grown locally, they were dirt-cheap. Triumphantly, I hurried back to the bus like a successful hunter-gatherer who had just saved his tribe from starvation. Bounding up the steps, I hoisted the bunch of bananas over my shoulders like a freshly killed wild boar and proudly hollered, "NINE CENTS A POUND!" The going rate was 65 cents a pound in northern Minnesota, so this was a major achievement for my dwindling supply of cash.

Fifty people packed the bus. Most were white, middle-aged, and alarmingly clean with light-colored slacks. One hundred eyes briefly stared at me like I had three heads, but I didn't care. With excitement I carried my prize to the back of the vehicle while passing a few out here and there like a proud new father might share cigars. Still left with 20 or more, I pounded several down in celebration. I tended to eat very poorly on this trip. These golden-colored and perfectly ripe bananas were just what the doctor ordered. With great contentment and satisfaction I nestled in to enjoy the view out my window. Slowly we approached what I felt was the heart of John Muir's world, Yosemite, which owes its existence as a national park to his dogged persistence.

I felt a special kinship with John Muir. He was possessed by a similar wanderlust, and was a Wisconsin boy, like me. He loved learning all he could about the natural world through experience and by living closely with it. His thirst for adventure and exploration was legendary. I sought to emulate his childlike wonder of nature and still endeavor to pass it on to my kids, because it points us to our Creator. During a violent thunderstorm, for example, you'd be more likely to find him outside enjoying the full fury of the storm rather than huddled under a quilt in fright. He was even known to climb high up into a tree so as to fully experience the gales. He also went on long journeys virtually unencumbered by any belongings, which at this point was especially appealing to me. Typically Mr. Muir carried only bread and tea for nourishment, a blanket, and the clothes on his back as he ventured deep into Yosemite country. While reading about him, my heart beat expectantly as the changes in topography announced our imminent arrival.

29

AN INAUSPICIOUS START

Arriving in Yosemite Valley, it was painfully obvious as we endured a lengthy traffic jam that this was not the same valley that once enchanted Muir. Thanksgiving weekend is surprisingly busy at the park. Nearly everyone stays within the seven-square-mile confines of the Valley where they are comfortably swaddled in considerable amenities. These include shuttle buses with regular stops throughout its length and breadth, a full array of shopping opportunities, hotels, restaurants, a gas station, post office, and more. It feels like a small city.

My first night was spent in the bowels of the Valley in a campground pockmarked by tents and humanity. It was reminiscent of a refugee camp. A minimum of six people shared each campsite, and I was beyond fortunate to be given the last available patch of dirt that measured some 20 square feet. Within a few feet in one direction I could distinctly hear people laughing loudly at private jokes. A tent erected an arm's length on the other side of me housed a young couple getting high in preparation for a marathon love-making session that seemed to stretch on interminably. This made concentration especially difficult for this young virgin cocooned nearby. A generator, or possibly an air compressor, at the gas station immediately adjacent to me contributed a steady beat to the cacophonous, unholy symphony.

I desperately wanted to peel on out of there, but needed to wait until 9:00 a.m. the following morning when the stores opened. I needed to resupply and obtain a permit. Once again, this was one major drawback to traveling by train. The options for replenishing supplies were very limited, and it was particularly painful to waste such precious daylight.

Another limiting factor in not having a car was that I could only travel by foot when on my own. This limited my options to say the least, although it allowed me to come to know a particular location extremely well. I planned on spending five days in the backcountry, so it was necessary to choose my general direction wisely. It would be impossible to backtrack from the north to the southern portions of the park if I changed my mind 20 miles into my journey, for example.

Compounding the issue immeasurably was the fact that the park rangers could offer no helpful advice to a backcountry traveler whatsoever. This problem isn't isolated to Yosemite, either. I have experienced this at numerous national and state parks, and even from the U.S. Forest Service. It seems that asking these friendly park rangers for advice can even result in a negative influence on one's journey. For the life of me, I don't know how or why they end up in these positions. One would think they'd be excited to explore the park during their downtime, but it's painfully obvious that all they want to do when they're off is get the hell out of Dodge. Frankly, the backcountry would accomplish just that. There are virtually no tourists out there. Why would you want to be a park ranger if you don't particularly enjoy the outdoors (as measured by how you spend your time)? I've never been able to figure this out, and challenge you to prove me wrong at a park near you. Ninety-nine percent of the time you will discover that they have almost no knowledge of their park outside of the well-worn areas that can be driven to or easily reached on a paved path with a dressed up Chihuahua in tow.

Ask the right questions, however, and they'll have a ready answer. Where are the bathrooms? How can I get to the High Falls? Answer, "Take the #6 shuttle that stops here 15 minutes after the hour." It is very depressing. These encounters let me down every time in a manner similar to discovering that the tooth fairy cares nothing for either teeth or children, but only for the commission she pockets for each gig. Sadly, I allow myself to be disappointed each time I visit a park as I hope that "just this once" somebody will have adventured more than a half mile into the interior.

This time was no different. Perhaps I should have designed my own journey by simply studying a topographic map of Yosemite. Of all the parks in the country I expected a better knowledge of the backcountry in this place that is a mecca to so many. At 19 years old I just didn't know any better. I still wish I could have passed between some of the sequoias that grow there, but instead I went to the northern portions of the park where there aren't any. This was before the Internet was widely known, so I had done no research of any of the places until I got there. The decision on a route was crucial because I wouldn't be able to simply hop in a car and go see something else if I were to tire of the scenery in a specific area.

All in all, though, I found not having a car to be extremely liberating. There were no breakdowns, maintenance issues, or gas station stops to worry about. More importantly, times of travel between destinations involved complete relaxation and rest.

After great delays that set me back considerably, I finally took leave of the throngs of people around lunchtime and hiked up and out of the Valley. I can't underscore enough how disappointing Yosemite Valley was. Even Yosemite Falls, touted as the highest waterfall in the world, was completely dried up. It was just a dark stain on the cliff!

30

YOSEMITE IN ALL ITS GLORY

With each passing step, I gained elevation, perspective, clarity, and higher spirits as I climbed high up into God's country. I was on my way to the Tuolumne meadows, which John Muir had praised, and possibly even the Grand Canyon of the Tuolumne (purportedly one of the deepest canyons in the world). The snows hadn't arrived yet, and this being the 25th of November they were rather late in coming. I was gravely warned that snow was in the forecast, and that two to four feet could easily fall higher up in the mountains. On the way. Overdue. Imminent. Looming. Images of the Donner Party—trapped in the mountains and reduced to cannibalism—sprang to mind. I was nervous and filled with a sense of foreboding, but it felt good to return to wilderness where I felt at home, and away from buses, restaurants, camcorder-toting tourists, noise, and distractions.

My pack increasingly weighed me down more and more. I clearly had packed too much. Lugging several heavy books along did not help! The climb was steep, strenuous, and difficult. Having left late in the day, I wasn't able to hike far enough to make it to a suitable campsite that night. I slept beneath a granite quarter dome a mile before Clouds Rest, a mountain at just under 10,000 feet that was Muir's favorite vantage point of his beloved Yosemite Valley. I slept on the side of the mountain at 8,700 feet of elevation, at a 25-degree angle. The sunset that night was incredible, and the panoramic view from that lofty height was fantastic. I enjoyed my first campfire of the trip that night, reading by it while hearing the serenade of yipping coyotes. I found turning in for the night while entirely alone in the mountains somewhat unnerving. I began a practice of urinating on the fire to create an awful stench that I hoped would keep predators away, and let loose a deep guttural roar that echoed across the opposing mountains in my best impersonation of a Sasquatch before climbing in to the safety of my tent.

That night there was a mixture of freezing rain and snow. I slept soundly, and was grateful to wake to a scant ground covering that would not prevent further travel. In the morning I made my usual oatmeal mush that provided little enjoyment without any sugar. I had forgotten to pack the condiment, and being basically a kid I never thought of simply buying some. After breaking down the camp I excitedly heaved that beast of a pack onto my shoulders for the climb ahead. It almost immediately sucked the energy out of me, as I was apparently becoming worn out. The half-inch of snow and ice made the hiking treacherous and slow. I looked forward to refilling my water at a nearby stream on the map, but it turned out to be completely dry (another victim of the drought). This became a theme, and it was hard to trust that rivers on the map actually existed.

The hike to the top of Clouds Rest was exceedingly steep. The peak itself was encased in a thin layer of ice that made traveling around on anything but all fours entirely perilous, but the view of Yosemite Valley and all its greenness was well worth the energy spent. El Capitan, the Yosemite Falls stain, Half Dome, and all the major landmarks are visible from up there without the malls and traffic.

At times portions of the trail were difficult to follow due to the small amount of snow that concealed the way. I kept a constant eye on the weather, and prayed for safety. I feared the prospect of being trapped up there in heavy snow, which once again should have already arrived by that point and was due at any time.

After getting past Clouds Rest I didn't see a single person until I returned to the Valley a few days later, which I found to be astounding. There had been many thousands of people crammed in like sardines down among the traffic jam that often defines that part of the park.

I felt thoroughly exhausted all day long due to my heavy pack that I grew to resent, and hiked just 12 to 13 miles that day. It felt every bit as difficult as traveling twice that distance, and the steep terrain contributed to the effect. Essentially having all of Yosemite to myself, the most visited national park in the country, was positively exhilarating though. There were numerous locations that afforded views for miles clear to the horizon, and there wasn't a sign of anybody in any direction.

They must have closed the road that travelled through that portion of the park for the season, because this was downright shocking. I couldn't see the road, but in other seasons hikers could park at nearby trailheads and not have to hike as far. Was everyone shopping?

Reaching an empty campground at May Lake, I selected a prime spot right on the water. What a precious commodity this was, and a marked contrast to my previous journey/swim through the wilderness of Olympic National Park. The sight of all this water in the middle of the park was very encouraging. I had completely run out of water while stepping over numerous dry streams that supposedly existed per the map. I learned from experience that the time between the melting of the previous year's snowpack and the new snows is a very dry period indeed.

The lake was nestled high in the mountains at 9,270 feet, with Mount Hoffman towering above it. I was really stunned and counted myself lucky to be camping that high up so late in November. In most years this would have been impossible with several feet of snow on the ground. Winter was in the air, though. The evening was chilly after I completed my nighttime ritual with the fire and terrifying roar.

The following morning I made a decision I would greatly regret. It still pulls me internally back to Yosemite, because I wasn't able to venture as far as I wanted as a result of it. I can't tell you how discouraging it can get to take down your tent in the morning, cram it all into the bag that is just a little too small if you fail to fold it as carefully as a Marine folds the flag, load everything into that bastardly torture device called a backpack, and due to shortened days set up and remake your campsite just eight hours later.

I had a guaranteed source of water at this beautiful mountain lake, and I just didn't feel like taking everything apart one more time. Neither my body nor my mind wanted to carry the burden any farther. Thus I left my campsite standing at the trusted water source and headed out lightly with only water, a small Gideon's New Testament, three granola bars, and my camera. I wore shorts along with a long-sleeve shirt to force me to keep moving, because I desperately wanted to see the Tuolumne.

Even though the highs remained in the 40's, the sun shined very brightly and kept me warm all day. Unfortunately this also contributed to my only serious impediment—chapped and blistered lips. I prayed as earnestly for Chapstick as I previously had beseeched the Almighty for deliverance from hypothermia in the Enchanted Valley. Alas, this was a prayer that was not to be answered as I wished. I would have to bear my cross. I never met another soul on the trail. I would have happily crossed a valley to a campsite far in the distance to pay someone $50 for their personal supply of lip balm. None fell out of the heavens either.

I trotted at a quick-time pace to the Glen Aulin camping area. This remarkable Garden of Eden was so delightful and pleasing to the eye that I was wishing I had brought all my belongings. I also carved out time to make a couple-mile incursion into the Tuolumne Meadows, which John Muir had relished. The scene was breathtaking with mountains of granite all around. Cathedral Peak, at nearly 11,000 feet, was especially prominent and grounded its surroundings in a manner similar to a white chapel within a quaint Vermont village.

Cathedral's spire pierced deeply into the blue sky. Being in the Tuolumne Meadows in the midst of all this splendor provoked unprompted worship. It was as if I had advanced to where mere mortals do not belong, and indeed there were no signs whatsoever of humanity. I experienced the majesty much as John Muir had 126 years earlier in 1869, who captures the scene nicely:

"I never weary gazing at the wonderful Cathedral. It has more individual character than any other rock or mountain I ever saw, excepting perhaps the Yosemite South Dome. This…is the first time I have been at church in California, led here at last, every door graciously opened for the poor lonely worshiper."

Due to waning daylight, I was not afforded the luxury of lingering. I had to constantly push myself so I would not be caught out alone in the mountains wearing shorts after dark when the temperature would plummet. In retrospect it was a bad idea, a potentially fatal rookie mistake, to trek so far from camp without warm clothes just in case. My body sure did appreciate the lightness though. I was now buoyant by comparison.

Though I knew the journey back would exhaust every second of daylight, I allowed myself ten minutes to recline along the Tuolumne River. I longed to spend the entire day in repose at this peaceful spot. It was already well into the afternoon, and I had a 10-mile hike back through extremely rugged terrain. It is profoundly difficult to pack a 20-25 mile hike into eight hours, and it demands that you don't put much thought into eating or breaks.

I rested along the river as the angling sun warmed the whole scene perfectly. Glen Aulin was lower in elevation than where I had camped at May Lake, and was therefore significantly warmer. It is located in a small meadow with trees nicely interspersed throughout. I was in a low spot that was heavenly. Waterfalls splashed down the steep mountain into a strikingly beautiful cerulean blue pool. The sun cast upon it in such a way as to render it Caribbean in character, and it felt tropical to me. I read a couple Psalms for a few minutes, soaked in every detail of the scene while desperately wishing I was making camp there, and prayed to give thanks that I had been kept safe thus far.

All summer this would have been a very crowded gathering spot for tourists, but I had many square miles to myself at the end of November. I listened to the soothing sounds of the river moving down the mountain in no particular hurry since it was so low. The wind rushed busily through the treetops while I was tucked into a protected alcove surveying my little kingdom. Finally I paid heed to the lowering sun, realizing that I desperately had to leave.

The hike back was a joyful forced march that was a kind of walk/run in my big clodhopper hiking boots. There was no time for stopping. I even continued a slow walk while urinating. Still, I drank in the beauty like a hummingbird sucking down nectar. The trail opened up on ridges to rapturous panoramic views. Spires of granite at opposite ends of my journey marked my progress from one end of the horizon to the other. At times I broke into an all-out run as the sun dipped further behind the mountains. The distance remained formidable. The last leg of the journey was entirely uphill, seemed to go on forever, and it was becoming mighty chilly with the elevation gain and increasing winds.

I made it back during the last waning moments of twilight following a gorgeous sunset, bundled up, and built a roaring fire in the dark to warm myself. For supper I pulled out some freeze-dried lasagna that made my badly blistered lips writhe in agony. This was the pain a slug must feel in its final death throes when doused with salt.

Incredibly, I had to cut my trip into the backcountry short by a full day because I didn't have $2 in Chapstick with me. Am I spokesman material or what? My lips were in such rotten shape that I couldn't even open my mouth wide enough to allow for the full entry of a spoonful of oatmeal in the morning. I'd force it through the cracked and bleeding lips to get some down my gullet, but much of it was scraped off the spoon by failing lips, unable to enter my body. The Bible speaks the truth in another context while admonishing, "When one part of the body hurts, the whole body hurts."

The hike from May Lake to the bottom of Yosemite Valley was epic in terms of the misery it meted out on my already pitiful state. I chose the shortest route on the map. At a distance of 15 mostly downhill miles it seemed this would be a simple promenade compared to other days. Perhaps a promenade on the deck of the Titanic!

I wearied greatly under the strain of constantly moving downhill, but the grade of the trail was relentless. The final descent into the Valley was on a trail that I wouldn't wish on my worst enemy. It's the only trail I've ever truly hated. That day I descended 5,500 feet in elevation, and half of this was virtually straight down through switchback on top of switchback (109 of them to be precise) over the last torturous mile. Awful doesn't begin to describe it, and I was in top-notch physical shape. My feet were beyond sore as blisters and hot spots burned with hellfire fury. I kept myself going by focusing my mind on how wonderful the fantastically cool waters of Mirror Lake at the bottom would feel on my feet.

The path was crazy-steep. To add to the fun, the trail was full of big rocks. Finding a single piece of soft dirt to plant my foot on was like finding the prize at the bottom of an enormous box of Cracker Jack. Many of these rocks were sharp and jagged at the top. I was forced to place each painful step on these while carefully trundling downward from rock to rock. Yeah, Hell on Earth. That's what it was. At one rest stop I realized in utter horror that I had left my camera ten switchbacks up, and seriously gave thought to leaving it there. Reluctantly, I lumbered back up to retrieve it.

The hot sun slowly cooked me in a rotisserie as I went round and round on the dizzying switchbacks. The high temperature in the Valley was just 54 degrees that day. After being in the cooler elevations it felt like I was entering into the gates of Hell with the intense sun. There's that word again. Hell, Hellfire, damnation, damned, burning misery. And no shade for relief.

With an elation that wasn't rivaled until my wedding night, I finally reached the bottom. Here the walk was steady on a flat-as-a-pancake horse trail. I was more than eager to cool my feet in the lake. After ten minutes of progress, and repeated stares at the map, I was dismayed to discover that I was already walking along what was apparently a good-sized lake. Now it was completely dried up as if I had entered an apocalypse. Hope was shattered as I stared in disbelief at the wasteland that was supposed to provide me relief. It looked like something akin to a salt flat. Lakes don't just dry up in a season where I'm from!

I took to walking from one pile of horse crap to another. The freshest, squishiest, and wettest piles of digested slop were the best. These felt pretty good, and were a welcome relief. I couldn't handle any more steps on hard surfaces.

I am one of those guys you see that is constantly toting around a water bottle. Curious people often ask the reason. Well, this is why. I have a profound aversion to thirst after these experiences. Even at home I'm uncomfortable if I don't have a quart of water sitting beside me, and never think of turning in for the night without a beautifully filled glass of water on my nightstand. I also use a clear glass. Lovely, clean, cool water is a marvelous thing. I never tire of seeing it.

Eventually I made it back to the congested part of the Valley that was filled to the brim with obnoxious people. Nobody even seemed to desire to leave the Valley as they visited stores and took in the major sites. They wore the look of people in a hurry; city people who hadn't slowed down enough to fully appreciate the park for what it really is. I found it impossible to understand why one would go through the time and expense of getting there, and then not get up and out of this gigantic staging area. It was shocking, quite a letdown actually, after having hundreds of square miles to myself. I just longed to be in the backcountry again.

I procured relief for my lips at one of the stores, and was stunned to discover that every single postcard contained scenes from within the Valley (a small portion of this very large park). After moping around I reluctantly plunked down $80 for a hotel room with walls so thin I could hear folks in both rooms on either side of me and all the cars on the busy street outside. I refused to spend another night in that crazy refugee camp.

There was so much more to experience in Yosemite, but I arranged a ride out the next day by calling Amtrak because I didn't wish to spend another full day in such conditions. I must say a lengthy soak in the bathtub felt marvelous on my aching body. I lit the room with my single candle lantern. Due to a maintenance issue there was no electricity in the building until 9 pm. Ironically, when the lights came on at that time, I was too tired to avail myself of the convenience of reading in a comfortable bed. Drifting into a deep sleep, I felt profoundly grateful for a marvelous introduction to Yosemite National Park. I was sure I'd be back some day. Eventually the prophecy will be fulfilled when my family joins me to recline along the Tuolumne River and to pass between sequoias that have thrived since the early days of the Roman Empire.

31

DOWN AND OUT AND UP AND ONWARD FROM THE GRAND CANYON

A profound sense of wonder beguiles most people as they approach the rim and gaze across the abyss of the Grand Canyon. Rapturous religious experiences bring some to tears as they are transported into the ethereal. I, on the other hand, was disappointed.

Peering over the railing at the South Rim showed a pretty enough canyon, but who hasn't already seen hundreds of pictures from this very spot? I saw no greenness or evidence of life. The large dust bowl wasn't nearly as grand as I had imagined. Perhaps damning my initial impressions were numerous buses and thousands of tourists sporting ill-fitting cowboy hats with camcorders capturing the panorama. The scene was reminiscent of a Republican national convention.

It is impossible for me to appreciate a view without becoming part of the landscape for a while and working with it. Every stretch of land has its own character. Being dropped off at an overlook prevents me from getting any sense of it.

I longed for the moisture and greenery of Washington or Minnesota, and missed friends after becoming travel-weary. I also felt increasingly out of place while heading south. My compass apparently points north. On the way to Arizona, in Los Angeles for example, I stuck out as a Midwestern boy among nicely dressed commuters.

It was the beginning of December, and I was ready to head home. I called Amtrak to shorten my stay by a day since I was so disappointed, which left me only three nights in the canyon. I then made the fatal mistake of asking park rangers for advice again, and wound up reserving all three nights at the Indian Garden camping area. It is dry and dusty, being halfway down to the bottom along the Bright Angel Trail. Don't get me wrong; it was pretty, but the Grand Canyon only gets more beautiful as you venture farther into it. After being alone in the backcountry, it was difficult to share space with crowds of people. A tap providing an ample supply of running water was particularly nice, though.

Using Indian Gardens as a base camp pales in comparison to being nestled along the mighty Colorado River underneath deciduous trees that thrive along its banks at the bottom of the canyon. As darkness settled in on that first night, a vast silence descended on the canyon as a bright moon rose. It became apparent that I shouldn't have sacrificed a day in this wonder of wonders.

On the ride to the South Rim from Flagstaff, while reading

the literature, I thought I'd try conquering the Grand Canyon by hiking to the North Rim and back. It wasn't until I got off the bus, and was somewhat disappointed by the size of it, that I chucked this somewhat arrogant idea (as if it would be another notch in my belt). Due to the sheer volume of visitors, about five million each year, park administrators are less open to whimsical on-the-fly plan making. Once your plans are made it is difficult to change them since there are no pay phones at the mile markers.

Being down in the canyon really helped me slow down and cooperate with this magnificent environment, rather than trying to conquer it. I learned to experience it with all my senses instead of simply seeing it. Each layer of geologic history presents its own surprises. They encourage a slower pace of life. The varieties of colors in the rocks are remarkable. The look and feel of the environment changes substantially at various times of day and light conditions. When I had arrived at midday, and viewed it from above, the sun was high. The harsh light washed out many colors and subtleties. Later and earlier in the day are the prime times as limitless shades of red, gray, white, and orange expose themselves for a time. The curtain of the stage almost imperceptibly raises and lowers an inch at a time as the spectacle goes on.

I awoke with eager expectation for my first full day of hiking, hoping to cover a lot of ground in a sort of blitzkrieg of the landscape. The morning began with an unexpected treat— sugar for my oatmeal! My neighbors gave me theirs along with a book. They were shedding weight for the hike out. For a small guy I certainly didn't put enough thought into the amount of pounds I carried. I'd end up leaving with six hefty books stacked in my pack. At the time I didn't care. For two full days I could explore with little more than the clothes on my back and some water.

I ventured down the less-frequently-travelled Tonto West Trail with my restless explorer tendency, wanting to see as much of this wonder of the world as I could. Planning on heading out as far as possible, I arrived at a fantastic view of the Colorado River gorge after traveling just six miles. I had arrived. This was enough. The serenity and beauty captivated me. Since I shortened my hike so much I was able to just sit and enjoy it for three amazing hours. I was in shorts and slightly chilled while sitting still, but the sun was warm and bright. I passed the time in the Gospel of Luke from my tiny Gideon's pocket Bible. It was all pretty new to me so I drank it in, meditating on the words as they ricocheted through my brains, guts, and soul like a ball in a pinball machine illuminating previously unlit areas. It felt as if I was actually able to communicate with the maker of this beautiful place. My prayers were like a continuous back and forth conversation.

I returned to my campsite changed. An epic sunset came and went. A peaceful stillness descended after the last of the hikers passed through. There was no wind in the canyon that evening. With no trees and leaves to rustle in any faint stray breeze, it was entirely silent. Everyone was respectful of the silence—in awe—and longed for it as much as me. I enjoyed a casual moonlit stroll without any need of a flashlight. My companion was the rapidly chilling night air that dipped into the 20s. The frost of my breath dispersed peacefully above the ancient canyon into the moon and star-lit heavens. This was illumination of the highest order. I can hardly conceive of how incredible the stars would be without a full moon, but the bright extraterrestrial light added a nice dimension as the place was lit surprisingly well. When I returned to my campsite I was even able to write in my journal with its aid.

The following day centered around a fantastic journey to the bottom of the canyon. The delightful walk ended anything that remained of my prejudices of it being just a huge dust bowl. I enjoyed the entire hike even more than the previous day's journey, though there were quite a few fellow pilgrims this time.

The trail follows Pipe Creek much of the way. It was wonderful to hear the river flow in this arid place. I observed that it brought the lifeblood for countless plants and animals. The rocks and canyon walls were very dark near the bottom. I visited Phantom Ranch along the Colorado River in the heart of the canyon, bought a Snickers bar for twice the going rate, and loved it. This would be an excellent destination for a family vacation someday. I mailed several postcards that were carried up by mule to the top of the canyon.

The Colorado River roared with might. Large, powerful eddy's swirled in the depths. Along the river, around the ranch and camping area I had bypassed, a surprising number of trees grew (cottonwoods mostly, but aspens as well). They were just hitting their peak fall colors in the beginning of December. It was a most welcome site after having journeyed from the border country of northern Minnesota where leaves had pretty much dropped by the end of September.

I greatly regretted not camping at the Bright Angel Campground down among all that beauty, but I spent a pleasant day following the river nonetheless. I made sure to head back to camp with time to spare, and found the trip up the canyon to my campsite at the midway point far less difficult than imagined. There was plenty of daylight to spare. The hike up from the Colorado River is definitely strenuous, and is marked with plentiful signs warning day hikers of the difficulty, but it hardly compared with hiking into and out of Yosemite Valley. It wasn't even in the same ballpark or league.

As I sat there taking in the sweeping breadth of the canyon from my campsite, I reveled in a whole new appreciation for its grandness and found it to be incredible. Getting below the surface of things, and really working to understand them has a way of doing this. It's entirely the same with people.

I reflected long into the night, my last. It had been my final day of exploration, adventure, and wandering. I found it hard to grasp, while sitting in the midst of the one and only Grand Canyon in Arizona, that in just three days I'd be returning home to lots of snow and below-zero temperatures. The time had flown by. I had a sense of how fortunate I was to enjoy this incredible month. It had been a once-in-a-lifetime, coming-of-age rite of passage. I felt sorry for kids my age that only knew the worlds of school and work. I had grown into a man on this journey. I was also grateful that my ongoing growth and education was continuing upon my return to the cabin in the wilderness. This was only the closing of a chapter in my quest. I wasn't facing a soul-jarring crash back into the status quo.

The next morning I packed up my tent for the last time. Every mundane act was filled with poignancy and meaning, but I was definitely ready to put my camping gear away for the season. I was so sick of packing everything by the end! Folding the tent perfectly, compressing the sleeping bag into its sack, cramming everything into my immense backpack that always had a way of being just 90 percent of the size I required, and other drudgeries were coming to an end. I was finally prepared to stop wandering and hole up for the winter.

I hiked out of the canyon unhurriedly, somewhat reluctantly, and in a contemplative mood. While on the trail I happened upon one of the friendliest and most generous individuals I've ever met. His name was Blair Larson, and he was several years older than me at around 25 years of age. It was a tremendous gift to have met him. Nearly two decades later I have the same sense of gratitude. Once again, never take for granted the power of one genuinely friendly encounter with a fellow human being.

It was absolutely wonderful to share the end of my journey with a friend rather than finish by plodding on alone. I bought him an ice cream cone at the top, and returned to discover an incredible sight that nearly brought me to tears. In a quiet area away from the crowds he was heating the entire contents of a quart jar of canned venison that he had carried with him all that way (from the top to the bottom, and back to the top again). We sat three feet from the steep cliff in a scene of majesty. We were part of the sublime heavenly setting. This wasn't just an overlook anymore. My DNA was left in the canyon, and a part of the canyon was in me. It was as if the deer had been sacrificed and was now being offered as a sweet-smelling burnt offering to the Maker of the Grand Canyon.

The venison was precious, artfully prepared a month earlier by Blair's mother. It was indescribably tender due to being canned. It melted in my mouth along with the rice and spices he combined it with. My belly beamed with satisfaction from this wild game taste-explosion. I had spent most of the past few weeks eating freeze-dried meals, granola bars, and bland unsweetened oatmeal. What a way to cap off a mind, heart, and soul-altering trip. The contrast in food quality, and the immediate infusion of energy this provided, also helped me understand the cause of the creeping lethargy that had beset me.

He then drove me to Flagstaff, and I enjoyed his company immensely. I was thankful to skip what would have been my last bus ride. The drive through wide-open country, and then past beautiful Humphrey's Peak, the highest point in Arizona at 12,637 feet, was breathtaking. I savored every last moment, knowing I was soon to spend nearly two days on the train.

Blair decided to split a cheap hotel room with me before pressing on to Death Valley. My half of the expense was just $12. Being mobile in the city in the company of a buddy was fantastic. This was not taken for granted. That night I devoured a banana split at Dairy Queen, a full pint of Ben and Jerry's ice cream, a chili cheese burrito, and a full pound of frozen peas. Yum! Since I knew I was too frugal to eat in Amtrak's expensive dining car, I loaded up on provisions for the journey home: a loaf of French bread, bananas, Oatmeal Creme Pies, peanut butter chocolate chip cookies, bagels, baby carrots, apples, jam, and licorice. I have never bought so much junk food in all my life.

The unexpected blessing of friendship with Blair was cause for celebration. The rare discovery of a kindred spirit always is, but was amplified exponentially in this moment that otherwise may have found me in unabated loneliness. I was excited to learn that he would be working at an environmental learning center just a couple hours from my cabin in northern Minnesota. We discussed winter camping together in the Boundary Waters, but never ended up seeing each other again. Even so, I count him as a lifelong friend with whom I hope to sit down and enjoy a beer someday.

At length we spoke of spiritual things. He espoused no faith or even a belief in God. It remains challenging to reflect on the kindness and generosity that he showered on me so effortlessly. There have been others like him over the years that have similarly blessed me. It seems that many of these unassuming people, who I'll pigeonhole by describing as agnostics, are more generous with their time and talents with me than this self-described Christian pilgrim is with them.

My great friend and neighbor, we'll call him Ted, comes to mind. Recently I lost my job. I had been a mere polyp deep in the bowels of Corporate America, and one day I was snipped off without warning. He has spent countless hours helping my family in practical ways with his carpentry skills. My wife is an artist. She has a major art show next week, and Ted devoted at least ten hours to working with me on framing her one-of-a-kind paintings. Once again, in a manner similar to Blair's, there were no strings attached and no guilt. He is one of the few boosters out there who whole-heartedly supports our family's goal of going our own way independent of the business world that often seems to have a callous approach in its dealings with humanity.

We are hopeful that part of our family's future success in achieving financial independence, in addition to my writing endeavors, will lie in my wife's career as an artist. Unfortunately I am completely unskilled in the art of framing. Ted saved the day by quickly framing a dozen works of art on short notice. His act of service is an investment into our family's economic engine.

I could provide numerous examples of Ted's generosity, which flow out of him naturally, as if from a deep well. He doesn't even bother to ponder the existence of God or a higher power. From where do these kindnesses spring? An entire book could be written in appreciation of similar individuals in my life. They challenge me in so many ways. Mainly I just find these guys fun to be around. Sometimes I wonder if I suffer from a spiritual defect that causes me to enjoy these individuals more than church people.

In some ways I would be a different person today if it weren't for Blair's gift of venison. Tangible acts like this are touching to the heart, and impact lives for good. I have learned more and more of this from my neighbors, such as Ted. None of them would describe themselves as evangelical Christians, but they are all like family to me. I can't imagine life without them. Returning home from a long trip to discover neighbors outside is like coming home to family. They have been with me through good times and bad, and their individual reactions to my unemployment have been tremendously encouraging. A beer and a listening ear are freely given as I air out concerns. A job painting a house and garage is provided to me with dignity, and isn't considered a handout. The overall effect is that I can let my guard down with them while carrying on as the plain old mess that I am. I love my non-religious neighbors because of their unearthly care for my family that has created a strong bond of friendship. They have become a hybrid—not simply friends or family, but both.

I seem to be more touched by simple kindnesses than the average person. My childhood was marked by long seasons that were virtually bereft of kindness or of people taking an interest in me. When I was finally cast into the world alone, such acts were like a match unexpectedly lighting up a dark room. I continue to delight in these. Genuine companionship tops the list.

That final night in Arizona, due to having a 5 a.m. date with the train, I slept incredibly restlessly. Every hour I awoke violently, kicked off the sheets in a surge of adrenaline, and leaped out of bed like I was a part of a special forces unit under attack while running across the room to check the time. During each of these episodes I was positive I had missed the train until I held the alarm clock in my hands to examine it carefully and discover that it was only 1:00, 2:00,

3:00…

32

EQUILIBRIUM AND PEACE

Boarding a train evokes excitement and anticipation. The atmosphere buzzed with electricity while I stood in the early morning darkness of the platform as the bright light of the locomotive approached the Flagstaff depot. I wasn't striking out for the great unknown this time, however. With considerable hesitation, I bade my adventure goodbye while beginning the long journey home.

Riding the rails through northern Arizona and New Mexico was exceedingly peaceful. It was the ideal setting for reflecting on the trip and on what lay ahead. This was Louis L'Amour country at its best. After recently finishing some of his books, I felt a close kinship to this land.

The changing terrain outside my window aroused an unending fascination in me. Mesas dotted the landscape of this sparsely populated country. Mountains loomed in the distance beyond incredibly wide-open spaces in an exotic world drenched in beauty and serenity. In Gallup, New Mexico, a member of the Navajo Nation gave a guided tour in the observation car until he departed in Albuquerque. The land was marked by both beauty and culture. When we crossed the continental divide I quietly absorbed every aspect of the landscape. I chewed and ruminated on every detail while realizing that this was going to be the high point of the two-day journey, in more ways than one, as we began the gradual descent toward Chicago.

The ride through Navajo country takes time. It comprises an area the size of West Virginia, and has an extremely low population density. At that time 250,000 Navajos resided there. The train rolls through remote areas unseen by cars traveling on highways. We were pulled alongside several cliff dwelling ruins and near Sky City, which was formerly the center of a long-lasting and ancient trading network. It remains the oldest continuously inhabited city in the United States, having housed residents for an entire millennium. Traditional ways amazingly live on in Navajo country. Even from the train one can still spot people living in impossibly old cliff dwellings with no modern conveniences. Many ancient Indian pueblos are visible from the tracks as well. Clickety clack, clickety clack..... On and on the train continued past several old Spanish missions, and the ruins of a Spanish fort dating to around the year 1700.

Running has always been a hallmark of the Navajo civilization. Its long history is rooted in the culture due to practical reasons. The most important of which is simply that it was the old way of delivering messages. The Navajo guide beamed with pride while explaining that his nation was home to several of the best high school running programs in the country. I think he may have gone a bit far in referring to them as having the top 10 running programs in the States, but they have certainly cracked the top 10. This is remarkable considering that poverty, obesity, unemployment, alcoholism, and other struggles are endemic on the reservation.

Crossing the Rio Grande valley, a mountain range to the south revealed itself in majesty. Finally the train turned farther to the north. The sunset that evening was one of the finest I have ever seen. As the sun dipped down in the west, the sky in the east grew scarlet red. Suddenly the colors unfurled in the east in earnest while simultaneously flooding across the sky. Gradually the western sky turned red. Pretty soon all four corners of the world were bleeding red. I was totally immersed by it on all sides. Chugging along in the glass-encased observation car, the only angle not fully engulfed in color was under my feet. Finally, all of the sky's energy and focus was directed to the west for the grand finale. The horizon exploded in color, containing various shades of red, orange, and yellow. After I thought it was finally over I looked up to gaze at a few clouds that glowed red like the dying coals of a fire.

I was on a high. Everything was pregnant with meaning and preciousness. That evening I was deeply touched by the movie shown in the lounge car. Though the title of the movie is beyond embarrassing, I am compelled to share the impressions recorded in my journal verbatim:

I just got done watching <u>A Little Princess</u>, and it is one of the best movies I have ever seen. Some of the themes included equality among races and classes. I just loved it. It was really powerful. I have to help people with this life.

As someone newly liberated from a feeling of being looked down upon all my life, the story resonated particularly powerfully.

Go ahead and laugh, but doesn't that sound far more pleasant than driving thousands of bleary-eyed miles on the Interstate? All my time alone, and rarely being in any kind of hurry, helped me slow down to a state of perfect equilibrium. I observed nearly everything, learned to appreciate all that I saw, and was very often touched by it. My senses and emotions were quickened, more perceptive, and heightened. All of me was fully alive.

33

THERE'S NO PLACE LIKE HOME

I obviously had to come back down to earth eventually. At 2:30 a.m., a commotion stirred me awake. People moved about restlessly. Annoyed, I yelled out, "Doesn't anyone sleep around here?"

Then the loud country music started, as if in reply. An elderly woman in her 80s was blasting the most annoying then-current country music you can imagine in her Walkman radio (this was the mid-1990s remember). If it had been reasonably good music, I might have laughed at the sight of this old lady cranking up the tunes in her headphones as if in rebellion. It was tuned to a radio station, so I optimistically figured that in no time we would be out of range. We were zipping along at a good clip through the plains at nearly 90 miles per hour.

Wrong! The sounds of Kickass Kansas Kountry seemed to carry on forever. Then I heard a voice distinctly say, "102.1

somethin' somethin' Kansas country with a frequency of 1 gabillion watts." That fired me up greatly. Mercifully, she detrained an hour later. Over that period she occasionally dozed with the music blasting her brains into smithereens. The bright reading light above her shone like a spotlight while she slept, as if she was working on a killer tan.

I dubbed this leg of the journey "Hell Ride '95." Shortly thereafter, a drug bust in the car behind me held us up in Kansas City for over an hour. This is the part of the trip we all arrive at sooner or later. I just wanted to get home.

As the train sat idling, someone urinated into the garbage can, adding an awesome aroma to the already-stale car. It was one of the older trains where the toilets open up and drop their untreated payloads directly onto the tracks below, so the bathrooms were locked at stops. Think about this the next time you're strolling down a pair of railroad tracks! In fairness to Amtrak, however, even at that time most of the rides were relatively clean and new.

At long last I reached Chicago, which necessitated the boarding of a commuter train that makes daily trips to Milwaukee carrying well-heeled business people. Formerly I would have felt naive, childish, and insecure by my appearance while nestled in next to a type-A businesswoman in a power suit. This time was different. I had experienced more than many people do in a lifetime, and was filled with a quietly calm confidence along with a sense of expectation.

I was eager to see my mom and share these incredible stories with her. Arriving at 6:30 p.m. in Sturtevant, Wisconsin, I was highly deflated when Enoch came to pick me up instead of Mom. Talk about a letdown! He didn't ask me one thing about the trip during the 15-minute drive home. There wasn't even a passing comment made in reference to this major life-altering voyage I had just completed. Instead he proceeded with diarrhea of the mouth as he carried on about computers and the wicked-good things he could do with them, and his boring job. For good measure, he peppered in the same ubiquitous complaints about my mom that I've heard for most of my life. These always included a litany of reasons why she would be far more financially secure if she just gave in and married him.

He is the sort of person who dominates every conversation, and all things around him, including people. For the first time I was free of his powers. I felt bad for Mom, though. She became little more than a marionette in his presence, as he pulled the strings. I spent a couple of the longest days of my life with the two of them, and didn't have a single moment of quality time with my mom. Not one.

Without even a trace of sadness, but with plenty of elation, I hopped in the car for the ten-hour drive to my real home in northern Minnesota. I was returning to my small cabin with no television, radio, or telephone, close to the Boundary Waters and near the deep woods of Canada. My excitement and zest for life returned. The contrast between Mother and me was stark. I beamed and bristled with life and love as I prepared to leave. She held back tears of sadness and despair.

In exhaustion I returned to Minnesota. I wasn't accustomed to driving for hours devoid of the freedom to walk around and read, like on the train. Several times I had to pull over for sleep because I was drifting off behind the wheel. I was only able to manage five or ten minutes of rest here and there, because it got down to -33°F that night. This was a 106-degree difference from a one-hour layover I had enjoyed in Albuquerque, New Mexico, which was the last time I had gotten off the train before Chicago. The last couple hours of driving along the north shore of Lake Superior were torturous in the middle of the night.

Snow had overwhelmed the landscape. More than I had ever seen! A buzz for encountering my first truly northern winter gradually grew and became my next source of highly anticipated adventure. I had learned that there are adventures lurking around virtually every corner. Only the boring allow themselves to remain in a state of boredom. I also anticipated returning to good friends. On my long solo trip I had missed sharing experiences with others. What a fantastic feeling it was to slowly turn down the narrow driveway while loudly crunching on the frigid snow, and finally shut off the engine. I had returned in one piece to my cabin in the woods. No other place on earth called me. I was home, and grateful for it.

34

WINTER IN THE BIG WOODS

I picked the mother of all winters to hole up in a cabin in northern Minnesota away from the normal cares and stresses of the "real world." The winter of 1995-96 went down as the coldest and snowiest on record to that point. When this occurs in border country it is worth noting. What passes for extreme elsewhere is often a daily occurrence in this frigid realm. For a boy from southern Wisconsin it was doubly extreme and marvelous. I relished each minute of it. Every winter of my life since, and no doubt for the rest of my life, is measured against this winter to determine its severity. It is my benchmark.

My cabin was located in a fairly remote setting well inland from the popular tourist town of Grand Marais and its quaint harbor on Lake Superior. A mere handful of alluring miles separated me from the Boundary Waters Canoe Area Wilderness, which lies astride the international border. I was also a 10-minute drive and a three-and-a-half mile hike from the tallest point in Minnesota, Eagle Mountain, which is located in this federally designated wilderness. From the top of this vantage point all you see are lakes and miles and miles of untouched forest.

Quiet. Marvelously silent. This is the hallmark of winter in the Northland. I had no access to television, and only three radio stations. One of these was a French-language channel from Thunder Bay, Ontario. The lack of listening options helped me abandon the radio altogether.

A month of riding the rails and exploring the west was the perfect preparation for the quiet of the north woods that awaited. My body and mind had finally slowed enough to appreciate silence. This noiselessness became a great symphony, one with many movements. On paper the train trip was the high point of my nine months away from the bustling world. However, in many ways the great hush of stillness had the greatest impact on my transformation inside the womb. I really do consider myself to have been in a womb as I was reknit together as a whole human being during this period. Often the changes were unnoticeable, but day-by-day and hour-by-hour I was rebuilt.

There were absolutely no interruptions. I had no phone. I received mail at the lodge on the days I worked. Whole days strung themselves together like pearls in which I received no "news." Major headlines were delivered by the wind. Opening the door in the morning I'd discover that a major snowstorm had blanketed the region. Headlining the gossip column were cheerful chickadees. Pileated woodpeckers— striking in appearance, nearly as large as a crow, and the type

Woody Woodpecker was patterned after—loudly hammered out a beat in the standing dead wood of the forest. On one exciting day in late January, I thrilled in cheering on competitors in the John Beargrease Sled Dog Marathon making their way across the lake in front of my cabin. Throughout the day and night they battled extreme wind chills approaching 70 degrees below zero on a brutal 500 mile course (years later it was shortened to 400 miles) paying tribute to the son of an Anishinabe chief who delivered the U.S. mail along a similar route during the last 20 years of the 19th century. John Beargrease had completed this trip weekly, with loads weighing as much as 700 pounds, by dog sled throughout the bitterly cold winters along incredibly rugged terrain.

If anyone wished to reach me they had to use the U.S. mail. This is the form of communication I most appreciate and trust to this day. Coming home from work with one or two letters in hand was a major event to be cherished. I eagerly anticipated receiving these dispatches from the outside world for weeks at a time. They were well worth the wait. I spent hours crafting letters in response as well. This caused my interest in writing to grow, and was ultimately the seed that grew into the book you now hold.

My appetite for reading good books became more voracious than ever. I could easily spend an entire day reading, followed by an hour or two of writing family or friends to tell them about it. The odd thing is that I usually snuggled up in the cabin on mild sunny days with temperatures in the teens or 20s. Bitterly cold days well below zero nearly always found me out in the woods experiencing the cold and loving the challenge. I took pride in my attire while swimming in a head-to-toe sea of wool, fully girded for the frigid blasts.

February 2, 1996 was the coldest day of the year. The mercury plunged all the way down to 60 degrees below zero at a weather station in a nearby community. This was the coldest temperature ever recorded in the continental United States at that time. Our thermometer corroborated the good news that we were about equally as cold. The high that day reached a balmy 36 degrees below zero. Weeks had strung together with the temperature never climbing above 0°F, and this was the climax.

The excitement was almost too much for me to bear. I donned my best wooly clothes for a big adventure: union suit, wool bib overalls, thick wool socks, Steger Mukluks for cozy feet, and a sheepskin hat with earflaps that tied under my chin. I thrilled in snowshoeing seven miles round-trip to the top of Minnesota on Eagle Mountain on the coldest day of winter ever recorded. This kind of thing still excites me. A difficult challenge is incredibly satisfying when you're well-prepared.

The snow was four to five feet deep in the woods. I cruised along at a steady reasonable pace with my snowshoes. The steeper inclines of the ascent, and later the descent, were more difficult to navigate. The snowshoes tended to slide at an angle into the snow, and I'd laughingly fall into the fluff all the way up to my neck. It helps to have a pair of ski poles along for such a thing. I was able to pole myself back up, after some struggle, back onto my two feet. With the cautiousness that comes after having kids, it seems outlandish that I ventured out on such day trips without notifying anybody. I also had no communication device for the journey. Getting stuck deep in the woods could have quickly resulted in freezing to death, but the thought never occurred to me. I never felt alone. I considered these journeys to be quality time with my father and protector. Major challenges that might bring some to tears would honestly make me laugh and trust in him. I didn't get to that point overnight. Perhaps I'm not even there now, but I had been through tremendous adventures with God in that season. He had proven himself faithful. Like a little child bouncing on a father's knee, I trusted and delighted in him.

At the top I sat in silence as a gentle breeze washed over me on top of the mountain. The wind chills were astronomical (somewhere around 80 below zero). I felt surprisingly comfortable due to all the exertion and the cozy wool that enshrouded me. It was a rather pleasant day, in fact. Bitter cold indeed, but the sun was out and it wasn't overly windy. As a result of this experience I remain highly motivated to get outside and feel eventful weather like bitter cold, blizzards, windy days, Nor'easter storms on Lake Superior with 15-foot waves crashing into shore, etc. Being out there alone in challenging weather causes your natural laziness to step aside as the stronger aspects of your character emerge.

Another frigid day found me cruising down Highway 1 on a return trip from Ely, Minnesota, with my roommate, Eric. The rugged and twisty thread through the wilderness was one continuous sheet of ice throughout the entire 68 miles from the former mining town all the way to Lake Superior. The hairpin turns, with rocks and trees hugging the shoulder closely, were particularly treacherous.

Having come through the curves unscathed, my confidence built as we continued along the relatively straight but slippery portion prior to the hardscrabble towns of Isabella and Finland. There are a series of several large humps, followed by significant dips. From the crest of one of the rises I observed steam rising up from the road far in the distance. Fearing this might mark the presence of a moose, I took my foot off the gas to coast down to a safer speed. Due to glare ice I wasn't comfortable with the idea of applying the brakes. We were traveling too fast for the conditions. The resulting experience became a metaphor for the coming-of-age total life overhaul that was taking place. A caterpillar-like metamorphosis doesn't seem to go far enough to describe the complete teardown and rebuilding of my existence.

Careening up and down the humps for perhaps a half-mile, as if on a thrilling roller coaster ride, we finally made out the shapes of three moose camped out on the highway licking salt. Still barreling toward disaster, since the half-ton behemoths had staked out positions with no interest in moving, I had to recklessly jam on the brakes in a nothing-to-lose Hail Mary of sorts. The car immediately entered a 400-degree spin while the immense beasts just stood there in dumbfounded amazement on their stilt-like legs as they towered over my small Honda Accord. While spinning like a Tilt-A-Whirl, we narrowly missed clipping one moose by mere inches as the front end came whipping around. Gradually the Lilliputian car came to rest between the other two majestic fully-grown moose. Not a one of them had budged the entire time! Eric shouted in exhilaration,

"WOOHOO! WOOOOOOO! WOOOOHOOOOOO!!!"

It was a miracle that we didn't collide with one of those big, magnificent, dumb beasts. We sat in stunned silence for a couple minutes while feeling like sardines in a can. The moose eventually slipped away, back into the forest under their own terms.

Car accidents involving moose are not mere fender-bender annoyances. They can easily result in serious injury or death because the tall spindly legs of the animal can cause the bulk of the creature to fall onto the passengers while caving in the vehicle. A full-grown Minnesota moose may stand over six feet tall at the shoulders and weigh between 1,000 and 1,200 pounds, while sporting a body up to ten feet long. These animals demand, and are given, respect. After coming out of such an event unscathed, my driving habits changed permanently.

This episode is emblematic of what this nine-month gestational rebirthing period was for me. I had jammed on the brakes of my life to avoid complete and utter destruction, and made a necessary course correction. Continuing forward at the same trajectory and speed would have been calamitous. Removing myself from the life of a student was the best decision I ever made. It allowed time for a solid foundation to be laid, upon which a new life was built.

This one winter in that cabin was so impactful that virtually all of the hobbies and interests that I hold dear to this day originated there. Focused, uninterrupted time spent doing virtually nothing but the things you love will do that for you.

Days and weeks slipped by without the distractions of email, telemarketers, or even worries about bills. I had no real expenses to concern me. The top drawer of my dresser was filled with nothing but cash from my tips in the restaurant. I used these dollar bills to pay my share of the rent.

This cash also went into an insatiably greedy propane tank. Money flew up a literal hole in the ceiling, as we burned up $400 in fuel in just three weeks. I arrived home one day to find Eric waist-deep in snow—keep in mind that he is Goliath-like in stature at nearly seven-feet in height—as he peered into the propane tank's gauge in disbelief while diagnosing the cause of our cabin's near-freezing temperature. The remainder of a stovepipe punctured the ceiling, the woodstove having previously been removed. The landlord assured us that the pipe was blocked up inside. Upon inspection with a broomstick, however, we determined this wasn't the case. Eric skillfully sealed up the bottom of the pipe with a blanket and plastic.

This was my first experience living in a home as an adult. With the benefit of hindsight, I can see I relied almost entirely on Eric for basic upkeep and to keep things humming along properly—things a child takes for granted. Though I was cheerful and fun to be around, my experience of "homemaking" made me a horrible roommate. This wore upon our friendship. Eric, normally easy-going, blew up at me one afternoon over my constant neglect of the dishes. He was infuriated over having to wash out pans, crusted over with my morning oatmeal, that I precariously stacked in the sink as I always had. This wasn't the last instance of friction I would have with roommates in the coming years. Old habits are hard to break. Basic principles of hygiene and neighborliness were entirely unknown to me. Perhaps this is why Eric and I haven't kept in touch.

Even so, I greatly enjoyed sharing the cabin with my older and wiser friend. Though our paths crossed less and less, I appreciated his presence that helped keep our ship rightly sailed. He handled problems unconventionally, addressing them head-on, without a tendency to complain. For example, after his truck failed to start one day, he dealt with this by trucking home loads of scrap wood from the lumber mill where he worked. Each morning he'd wake up at 3:00 a.m. to start large bonfires in the snow just five feet from the grill of his truck, in an effort to warm the engine block enough to keep the oil moving in temperatures of -40°F to even -50°F. Morning after morning he'd crawl back into bed for a couple more hours of sleep. Eric made it through the difficult winter with grit and determination. He didn't have the luxury of leisure and adventure during this season, as I did. Exhaustion, mindless work, and a dearth of stimulating conversation seemed to carry him in another direction. I remain grateful that he took me in as a roommate. This was my first experience of a functioning home with adequate seating arrangements, rooms that were all accessible, and a kitchen that wasn't so filthy and cluttered that it was functionally useless.

I remained a challenging roommate for years. In college, for instance, 100% of the floor space in my room was covered with papers. Somehow I intuitively knew where important papers were located in my "filing system." Walking across my floor was like walking across hot coals as the papers crinkled under my feet. Organization simply meant keeping everything out so I could locate them. I was entirely clueless in how to otherwise put my belongings into order. I lost friends because of this. Each relationship, such as with Eric, was submerged under my carelessness. They did, however, provide stepping-stones upon which I eventually hopped across a perilous lagoon. If it weren't for the painful lessons learned through lost friendships, I doubt my ongoing marriage and family life would have continued on as successfully as it has. This isn't to say that there haven't been significant bumps along the way, though.

35

EMANCIPATED

Instead of exchanging the usual pleasantries after they made the ten-hour drive north, Enoch launched into a blowout of an argument as an opening salvo in a "first-strike" mentality. He virtually forced his way into my cabin while shouting that I was hurting my mom by skipping out on school. I would certainly never go back, and my life would amount to nothing as a result. A screaming match ensued for 20 minutes between the two main men in Mom's life that was not unlike the head butts of bighorn sheep in a final no-holds-barred life-or-death battle between us. Frozen in stunned disbelief, the eyes of my roommate became as wide as teacup saucers.

When the fireworks died down I told them to leave if this was why they had come. During this time in the cabin I was fully independent. Reveling in liberation from his domination for the first time, I simply could ask them to go back home if I didn't feel like being bullied. In a valiant show of resolve, Mom salvaged the situation. Ultimately we had a pleasant visit celebrating the holidays together. Thankfully they stayed in a cabin at the lodge 15 to 20 miles away. This provided necessary space between us. It had become impossible for the three of us to be confined between the same four walls for long.

My freedom was complete. I could no longer be forced to go wherever he and Mom wished, while enduring terror with him behind the wheel. A fork in the road had appeared, and I took a different path. "Free at last. Free at last. Thank God Almighty, I am free at last!" This is not hyperbole, but exactly how I felt. My sense of freedom, liberation, unshackling, and deliverance, cannot be underscored enough so it bears repeating. I was like the Israelite children being led out of bondage in Egypt.

It took time for Mom to see the wisdom in taking a break from college. I delight in sharing my story with college-age students experiencing a similar need for growth outside of an institution like a university. So many millions are confined to an environment that is stifling their development, but they remain due to family and societal pressures. I counsel these individuals who have only experienced a subtle taste of the freedom that adulthood brings to think outside of the box. Those that feel an inner sense of dissatisfaction would do well to consider stepping out from the assembly line that focuses on making good corporate workers. There is plenty of time to go back to that if one chooses.

Until you do this, it is difficult to comprehend just how counter-cultural it is to step away from the status quo of a career path that runs through college. I only removed myself for nine months, but others might consider a year or two to really immerse themselves in what they love. Perhaps forever. After he or she makes this decision they must remain resolute. Do not seek too much advice from others. It's shocking how many people are under the impression that you're throwing your life away, but the reverse is true. You might actually gain a full and abundant life. Your dreams will become more clear. You will be able to more adequately focus your life on pursuing them. It will help to chuck your cell phone. Use pencil and paper for communication, or you'll be inundated with "helpful" concerns every day. It is impossible to clear your head when faced with such an onslaught of advice.

This must be considered a serious, and yet joyous, quest. The pilgrim must not spend all their time in a dumb job while living at home. Expenses and work hours should be kept to a minimum so a surplus of leisure will exist. Additionally, the seeker would do well by not spending all their free time with old friends. They absolutely must break away to pursue new influences that soften their rough edges and contours. Far too many make the fatal error of working 40 hours a week to make a buck, and partying with the same stale crowd at night. This is a complete waste of precious time. Most of us have just a few years of untethered freedom before marrying and taking on responsibilities that will last a lifetime. Remember, it's your life and not anybody else's. Seize the day!

36

UNRELENTING JOY AND PEACE AS WINTER CONTINUES

Briggs, my roommate's golden retriever, and I snowshoed across Gunflint Lake to Canada one fine day. Hills, cliffs, and rock outcroppings surround the lake, providing visual interest. In winter it is especially beautiful and tranquil. The waters, being above the Laurentian Divide, drain north to Hudson Bay. It is also part of the border with Canada, so that was part of the draw for me.

This was years before concerns about border security reached stratospheric heights. I thought nothing of crossing the lake into Ontario for a picnic and some exploring. Though it was a frigid below-zero day, I encountered slush right in the middle of the lake—always disconcerting, to say the least. The snow conceals and insulates slushy water trapped above the ice. Crushing through the outer crust of insulating snow, you are suddenly greeted with the sensation of hitting water. For me this comes with a feeling of doom that a splashdown through apparently thin ice is imminent. In this case there was likely an ice depth of four feet or more below the slush. The experience can be alarmingly scary for me, because it always seems to happen far from shore, where I feel most vulnerable.

My daypack was unusually heavy as well. I was toting along a large cast iron skillet that was a gift from my grandma. Also inside were some diced potatoes and hamburger for a warm lunch. I built a fire on balsam bows laid directly on the deep snowpack high atop a rocky outcropping on the Canadian side of the lake. The prominent location allowed for a splendid view of the scenery as I spent an hour cooking my meal and enjoying the fire.

The Ontario side of Gunflint Lake is pure wilderness. Previously, it was home to a settlement of Native Americans, but in recent decades only one holdout remained—Charlie Cook. When I was there in early 1996, the Indian gentleman was 97 years old. He lived year-round in a shack until just the year before I had arrived. Due to his advanced age he had begun using it as his summer home because of the obvious hardships of living cut off from society during the harsh winters. After tromping around for a while on snowshoes, with Briggs bounding and cheerfully lunging through the deep snow ahead of me, I was thrilled to find Charlie's wilderness home.

When I was there as a 19-year-old budding explorer, memories of similar old timers who lived far off in the wilderness for much of the 20th century were still alive and vivid among large segments of the populace. A few pioneering legends, such as Justine Kerfoot (who was a good friend of Charlie's and lived across from him on Gunflint Lake for decades), were still alive as well. Dorothy Molter, the famous Root Beer Lady, had died just ten years earlier. She was the last full-time resident to have been allowed to live within the Boundary Waters Canoe Area Wilderness, an area three times the size of the state of Rhode Island. After her small resort on Knife Lake was shut down, she subsisted on the "donations" made by passing canoeists who enjoyed the famous root beer that she bottled herself and cooled with ice cut from the lake in winter and stored in an icehouse. Her legendary battle with the U.S. Forest Service to remain in her home after the land was federally designated a wilderness area gave her national prominence, which galvanized the public support she needed. Right up to the very end she lived 15 miles by canoe across several lakes and five portages from the nearest road, and 36 miles from the town of Ely. It was not difficult to come across individuals who knew these resilient and fiercely independent old timers, or at least had a passing acquaintance with them. The stories they told fueled my imagination of a life spent in the wilderness. Even though I ultimately chose having a family and another lifestyle, I have always found the lives of these hardscrabble people to be endlessly fascinating and inspiring.

Throughout the long winter my body, mind, and soul gradually slowed down to a point of virtual timelessness. Rare was the moment when I succumbed to any pressure concerning time. I followed my body's natural rhythms for a schedule. I enjoyed rejuvenating naps when tired, engaged in strenuous activities outdoors when my body and mind needed it, and relaxed whenever it struck my fancy. And, yes, it was necessary to go to work at set times.

However, my attitude toward time changed. I was no longer a slave to it. I lived fully in the moment without experiencing angst about the future or what I wanted to accomplish. I simply enjoyed whatever I was doing with the benefit of a mind that was not constantly multi-tasking or imagining what I would rather be doing instead. Mundane tasks, such as waiting for several hours in a dirty car repair shop, did not bother me. I always had plenty of books to dive into. Each moment that came and went was cherished. This has not been a self-perpetuating state of being that carries on regardless of any bad habits that may creep in occasionally, but the wisdom gained shaped my understanding of time forever. As much as possible I continue to eschew time pressures so as to more fully live in each moment. I scrawled "Embrace Timelessness" on my tip bucket in the restaurant, where pressure certainly mounted as a waiter on busy days. Being fully present in every task helped me maintain my equilibrium at these times.

One day in the restaurant stands out in particular. I opened the place up at 7:00 a.m. and sat there alone without a single customer until near the end of my shift at 3:00 p.m. The one individual to cross the threshold ordered a basket of french fries, stayed an hour, and left a tip of 85 cents. Minimum wage was just $4.25 at the time, but I didn't stress over the loss of income. It was a memorable and remarkably satisfying day. I passed most of it by reading a fantastically enjoyable biography of Dorothy Molter, *Root Beer Lady*, from cover to cover, which I obtained from the gift shop. I thrived by keeping my mind and imagination engaged throughout whatever circumstances came my way.

It could also be dead for half the day, and then without warning a senior citizen tour bus might show up. During the offseason only one waiter was kept on duty at a time mid-week. On those days I did everything but cook the food. This included hosting duties, running the cashier, taking orders, serving, washing dishes, clearing and setting tables, cleaning and monitoring supplies in the bathrooms, and keeping the gift shop tidy. A sudden influx of 45 hungry senior citizens was a real shock to the system, but they made the time pass quickly. I was thankful for a reduced workload of around four days per week, but on most days I appreciated a relaxed work environment that provided the opportunity to interact with a wide variety of people who passed through.

A frenetic pace of life spent constantly racing from one activity to another is not something I wish to pass on to my children. My wife and I endeavor to live intentionally, slowly, so as to be afforded the opportunity to welcome happy interruptions opportunistically rather than with annoyance (such as a visit with a neighbor on the bench in our front yard). I credit my months up north, far away from deadlines and an onslaught of meaningless activities, for what is certainly a mature understanding of time that many people fail to grasp until death or disease.

Insignificant trifles only serve to eat time corrosively, like rust. Climbers of corporate ladders often miss this on their ascent to dizzying heights. This one lasting lesson may have been my main takeaway from this time of rebirth. Real life skills like this that lead toward a healthier life and family over the duration of one's earthly existence is argument number one for a young person to take meaningful time off from school.

Additionally, I was infused with a greater zest for life and a sense of aliveness than ever before. Childlike wonder seeped into my mind and soul, as I became a whole person. Children are born with this sense of wonder, excitement, and an awareness of their environment. As Sigurd Olson observes in his book, *Reflections from the North Country*, "It can be nurtured and enhanced, but one must never allow knowledge to destroy its primitive delight." As a biology major during my freshman year of college, this is exactly what happened to me. It is worth learning as much as possible, but I agree with Sig that, "Too much attention to scientific detail can rob one of awareness and deeper meanings." My loss of wonder didn't just have to do with education and scientific detail, of course, but also with a lack of any kind of grounding coupled with a complete lack of purpose.

Grounding and a sense of rootedness came from gaining faith, knowledge, and coming to know God. A natural by-product of this was also a sense of connection to the land and the creatures he has made. My appreciation for his handiwork in creation widened with the horizons, which helped me to know my creator better as well, creating a sort of continuous loop that feeds itself.

Where once I was afraid of silence, I grew to thrive in it. Sigurd Olson explores this topic with eloquence. Reflecting back upon decades of experience, he wrote, "The silence itself was beyond the ordinary sounds of nature; it dealt with distance, timelessness, and perception, a sense of being engulfed in something greater where minor sounds were only a part, a hush embedded in our consciousness." Silence and solitude were embraced as I learned to slow down to live and love each and every moment while experiencing it, rather than constantly striving for more spectacular experiences in the future.

Awareness, wonder, perception, delight, joy, enthusiasm, enlivened senses, love, and a reason for living (and living well) were all included in the price of admission. Sunsets, delighting in literature, hiking, exploring wilderness, and virtually anything else, were all enjoyed as if I was experiencing them for the first time. In a sense I was. For the first time in my life I was truly alive.

37

METAMORPHED, THE BUTTERFLY FLUTTERS BACK TO SCHOOL

By removing distractions and broadening my focus outward instead of on my own problems, I discovered how simple (not mistaken for easy) it was to have knowledge of, and possess the keys to, a joy-filled life. My entire life had been torn down and reconstructed from scratch upon a solid foundation. I had come to know God intimately, and marveled at his signature in all things. There was no dichotomy between the spiritual and material. No line delineated sacred versus secular. Everything was sacred.

I learned to confide in people who built me up rather than tore me down. In the past, the "beautiful" people I sought out could be downright mean. Our concept of beauty is wildly skewed by an unhealthy infatuation with Hollywood celebrities. I was not among the chosen few, as they define it, but who is? Perhaps five percent of the population? Look around yourself from time to time to pleasantly discover that most people are not perfectly proportioned with gorgeous hair and features. As nearly all of us realize intuitively, unrealistic cultural expectations have disfigured our concepts of beauty and goodness.

Trying to fit in with the popular, elite, and outwardly beautiful people nearly destroyed me. Learning to find friends who appreciated me for who I had become was revolutionary. If it meant I would be alone occasionally, that was just fine. In fact, I grew to cherish these times of solitude. Constantly jockeying for position socially was exhaustingly soul-sucking because I had been living a lie by trying to be someone I wasn't (or even interested in). By tapping into the Source and shining from the inside out I became one of the real beautiful people. Nobody ever tells me that, or probably even thinks such foolishness, but I learned this is a state of mind that is not dependent on what the crowd thinks.

Being comfortable with who you are, and having an idea of your place in the world with a purpose, is no small matter. The shackles and fear of loneliness were forever cast away. I was able to spend extravagant amounts of time alone without feeling like a loser, and learned to thrive in solitude while truly hearing silence. This knowledge, and sharply honed skill, will continue to pay dividends throughout my life. Of course, this is just the tip of the iceberg. It is indicative of the lasting and remarkable metamorphosis that occurred by simply removing myself from school for the relatively short period of nine months. This time was absolutely gestational. I was honestly born anew. I highly recommend such a sabbatical to you, whether you need a full rebirthing or not.

My time away from school wasn't even a full year, but this break was long enough for a new course to be charted. When my time was up, it was completely obvious. The experience was similar to my longing to reach home during that last full day on the train. Four shifts in a row in the restaurant ended with me begrudgingly splashing through an overflow of brown sewage water in order to enter the women's restroom and plunge a blocked-up toilet. The disgusting scene played out each day with no end in sight—which included small gobs of goo splashed onto my black leather shoes—and was more than even my new positive attitude could handle. I was done. All that I had learned, experienced, and accomplished, had already greatly exceeded my expectations. It was time.

Though I anticipated significant culture shock, and I knew I'd need to adjust my mindset, I was ready to go back to school. I made just one more road trip to Colorado with my good friend, Mel Welch, in order to maximize the last few days of my sabbatical and to aid the transition. Then I returned to classes confident in my identity and who I was made to be. I was marked by joy, peace, and true equilibrium for the first time. I was content, took each day as it came, and felt like the richest man on earth.

38

THE GREAT OOZE OF 2000

A college education, my first experience of being loved and touched by the opposite sex, and four years had passed. Shawna, my beautiful wife, now lay passed out in my arms on the floor of the locked women's bathroom. We were at a gas station on 7 Mile Road. The somewhat dirty restroom lay across the street from the same 7 Mile Fair mentioned earlier, where I rode my bike to purchase many of the avian friends that were released into my bedroom bird sanctuary. Thus, we were only a few miles from my childhood home. A mere four miles had stretched into 400 light years.

The condition of Mom's house causes a monumental inconvenience at a time like this. My wife and I were newlyweds, only one year into marriage, and were in the process of moving across the country to Boston, Massachusetts, for graduate school. Rather than enjoy a relaxing visit in a comfortable home seven hours into a cross-country journey, like everyone else would, we arranged a more formal meeting at a Perkins Restaurant a few miles away along the freeway. The collection of dinner guests had never before been gathered around a single table. Remarkably, these included Mom, Enoch, and my dad. The intensity of the gathering created so many awkward moments that exuded copious amounts of stress that using a reference point in the Yalta Conference near the end of World War II pales in comparison. The latter's meeting of Churchill, Roosevelt, and Stalin seems like a picnic involving Brainy Smurf, Dreamy Smurf, and Grouchy Smurf. There really is that much bad blood between these three. Having them all at one table gave me wild heart palpitations and acid reflux.

Leaving the Perkins was profoundly relieving, but my wife endured a gauntlet of backslaps during repeated hugs. A swollen and infected cyst on Shawna's back burst a few miles down the Interstate. So here we were just four miles from Mom's house, fittingly situated adjacent to the largest flea market in the state of Wisconsin. The floor of a lady's room in a truck stop was preferable to limping over to the dirty and cluttered house that was bereft of a single place to sit. "Dirty" and "cluttered" are not synonyms here, either. The house is filthy, unhygienic, and an actual biohazard. This is no place for someone with an open wound to stretch out and be tended to. It festered the sort of conditions that caused people to die from minor surgeries in hospitals in the 19th century. It was a miserable feeling to deny my wife the kind of care she needed.

Instead, we sat on the floor of the locked women's restroom for the next 20 minutes. Among tears and confusion, an endlessly oozing supply of pus exhausted the entire supply of gauze pads from the first aid kit I obtained from the gas station attendant. I had to leave the bathroom to purchase more, in fact. After the wound was finally dressed, we hit the road for several more hours. Neither of us could believe what had happened, nor the irony of the location. That evening we spent the night in a cheap hotel, which came equipped with small rodents, in a bad neighborhood in northwest Indiana. I wish more than anything that I could have delivered a clean home and a mother's touch for my young wife that night.

Perhaps if I wish hard enough…

Nope, it still isn't happening.

39

MY BRIDE'S EXPERIENCE DOWN THE RABBIT HOLE

Daily I called her, seeking comfort. I was home for several days during a holiday break from college. I complained about the mess, desperately attempting to connect on an issue that nobody could possibly relate to. The exchanges went like this:

"There are all these boxes in my room. They're everywhere, and I'm so depressed."

Not understanding, she'd say, "You should read a book."

"Ugh… It's just not the kind of place where you want to read a book. I'm so bored, and there's nothing to do…"

Shawna was my first girlfriend, and quickly became my chief comforter and confidante. However, she still didn't come close to grasping the gravity of the situation. Nobody ever does until they see it for themselves. Seeing the mess and experiencing it, really living within it, are two different things. Thus, I've never really had anybody to fully relate to on these matters. If only I had a brother or sister to swap stories with, share complaints, or discuss strategies for Mom's future.

My future wife attempted to relate over the phone, as most people do, by saying something like, "My grandpa is a real packrat. You should see his basement!" Her preconceived ideas about the house and my stories were wildly off the mark. We drew closer together than ever when one day she saw for herself that my stories weren't exaggerated in any way, shape, or form.

Following our engagement to be married, the two of us went on a barnstorming tour so members of my family could meet her. Our first stop was Mom's house. Stories from this trip, as told by my wife and seen through her eyes, are endlessly entertaining for me. They are both hilarious and vindicating. It's gratifying to hear someone else's perspective on it for the first time. As a general rule I kept everyone out of there. Due to the absence of any siblings, this one experience with my wife that lasted a single night is all I have as a shared remembrance of the place with someone else acting as an objective third party.

I counseled her on the condition of the house during the long drive. We paused in the driveway before reluctantly opening the doors, as I reminded her that the dwelling was far worse than she could ever imagine. Once again I told her that every single time I enter the home, it is quite literally the worst I've ever seen it. It wasn't until we opened the door that she grasped in horror the full reality. There wasn't a single place to sit down. The stench overwhelmed her. To her credit, she managed a smile while warmly embracing my mom to keep from offending her.

I scraped off a place to sleep on the couch, and Shawna endured a horrid night's "rest" on the bed in my former bedroom. The entire time she worried about bugs crawling all over her, and was in a panic over the condition of the sheets. She remained in the center of the bed, afraid to be close to any wall or edge. It's hard to believe, but she insists that there were seed remnants in the sheets from my birds. The curtains immediately adjacent to her, draped alongside the bed, gave a whole new meaning to "window treatment." They remained festooned with bird poop a half decade after the last bird had flown the coop.

When the sun finally rose, in mercy, she emerged from the room after having done battle with its demons all night long. Warmly, I greeted her saying, "Well, do you want something to eat? I think there's a box of Lucky Charms around here or something." We chuckled at the notion. I knew darn well she would not be eating anything that came out of that kitchen. She had just emerged from the bathroom, closing the lid on a toilet that was completely blackened on the inside. Feeling filthy from having slept in my room, she mustered the courage to take a shower. The tub was completely lined with hair and filth, and the shower curtain was moldy. I frequently forget she actually stood naked in that narrow disgusting place, incredulously asking, "You actually did that???" Her reply goes, as she shivers in disgust, "BLEH… I DID!"

That morning we quickly decided to spend the next evening at my dad's. He resided in an apartment that was part of a housing project in Milwaukee, where his rent was generously subsidized. From Shawna's perspective, the relatively clean hardwood floor she slept on was like staying at the Ritz Carlton in comparison. Dad's French toast in the morning made the experience feel like a quaint bed and breakfast.

We returned a few years later to help Mom clean. Memories of that experience cause Shawna to remain horrified that she once slept there. This time we shelled out the expense of a hotel room for three days. I made Mom promise to arrange for a large dumpster to be dropped off in the front yard prior to our arrival. Daily I called her to check on the status during the week before our arrival. She lied repeatedly, saying there were no dumpsters available. Without hesitation I told her this was a lie, and that I was positive I could find one for her inside of ten minutes. She promised to try harder. The morning we left for the long drive she swore there would be a dumpster there, and even after we arrived she persisted in the lie. I could go on and on about the lying. Once again, compulsive lying and compulsive hoarding remain cheerful bedfellows within her. She can't help it.

As Shawna and I sat in the driveway, I counseled her once again that every time I arrive at the house it's the worst I've ever seen it. Even though my mom had been telling me daily that the house would be much cleaner this time, I knew this was a lie. She takes pride in hauling three garbage bags of unwanted items to Goodwill each week, and honestly believes this is making progress. The reality is that her efforts weren't even making a dent. The situation required a 40-yard dumpster, shovels, elbow grease, and a minimum of decision-making. My statement unfortunately proved accurate once again. The front door could only open halfway. The two of us stood at the threshold in disbelief. Not only was there not a single place to sit down, but the long-established paths had been consumed entirely by the blob. We were forced to climb a veritable mountain that was over our heads and practically rappel down the other side just to get into and out of the "living room."

We had attempted to swoop in and save the day for her. Quickly we learned this isn't possible. Shawna and I must have hauled out over a hundred large garbage bags for disposal. Mom went through them all while becoming emotionally unhinged and impossible to work with. It was also more than my young wife could handle adequately. She did her best, but is a bit squeamish even in ordinary settings. Add in a myriad of creepy crawlies, seen and unseen, and you have a recipe that she is incapable of stomaching. For example, she repeatedly stumbled across mummified mice in various states of decomposition. This required calling me over to handle disposal of the rodent. Sometimes it would mercifully just be a tail protruding from the bottom of a pile that resulted in a scream from Shawna. In stunned disbelief she came across a sealed package of raw bacon that had apparently been entombed for years, as if in a landfill. Her curiosity getting the best of her, she turned it over to discover another rotted mouse. From that moment on it was necessary for her to work outside where there was certainly plenty to do. We set up a large staging area for organizing items into boxes. Many of these went into various storage units, unseen, for years.

The house vomited and belched items throughout the front yard and driveway. Walking back and forth from the house to the staging areas outside with a dust mask firmly in place, I felt deeply embarrassed in the presence of neighbors I had once known. I didn't exchange pleasantries with anybody due to this, and also because I had a sense that this would be one last chance to get my mom's life in order so she could finally move. As the remaining hours of our stay ticked away, I worked at a feverish pace. We fell short, but gratefully fled the scene when it was time to return home to Duluth, Minnesota.

Now Shawna understands a bit of what it is like to spend a few days or a lifetime there. Mired is the word for it. No creativity can possibly be birthed there. One's senses are assaulted at all levels to the point of overload through permeating odor, overwhelming sights, the sensation of filth from the bottom of your feet to the top of your head, odd sounds, and even the taste that sticks to the roof of your mouth that I can only inadequately compare to the disgusting taste that endures after smoking a cheap cigar.

My mother chooses to continue living in that hellhole of extreme wretchedness and squalor every day of her life. This is not what I want for Mom. I'm powerless to rescue her. Now that she has reached retirement age she wants to get out from under the weight of her home, but is unable to make the difficult choices that are required. Wanting and doing are vastly different frames of mind, separated by a vast uncrossable chasm. Will she be trapped forever?

About a dozen years ago, when the problem of compulsive

hoarding was just beginning to receive the nation's attention, I eagerly tuned in to a show hosted by Oprah Winfrey on the topic. My excitement and anticipation for the upcoming program can hardly be overstated. It was akin to the Green Bay Packers, my favorite team, making it to the Super Bowl. I had never met anyone who grew up in conditions like mine, and never found a single individual who could fully relate to me on the subject. As the show started I expected to see images of homes as bad or worse than my mom's. Was I ever disappointed.

My mother could have easily highlighted this program that served to expose how much more common this problem is than I had realized. Footage of four homes was shown, and counseling was given to the occupants who all suffered from varying degrees of obsessive compulsive disorder (OCD), which was then a new term for me. None of these people who were shown on national television even came close to the problem that beset my mom. This caused me to despair that there was perhaps nobody in the world struggling with such a severe case of compulsive hoarding.

Television programs would later be created that were wholly devoted to the topic, such as *Buried Alive*, which make it clear that Mom isn't the only one in her shoes. Long-term counseling and medication are needed. I fear these will forever be avoided. She is not able to grasp the full scope of her disorder. Mom lives a life of isolation that very few people can even imagine. She lives in a prison constructed by her own two hands, day after day enduring the endless accusations her mountains of possessions must create in her mind. I hope this honest account will be a shot across the bow that she needs, not unlike the shock induced by the paddles used to restart a heart in cardiac arrest, to salvage her sunset years so she can live the kind of life most people take for granted.

40

MY CHILDREN STARE INTO AN ALIEN WORLD

Entering the children's area of the Milwaukee County Zoo, centered around a vast bowl of newly sealed asphalt, was like entering the caldera of a volcano. The sun beat down without even a slight wisp of a cloud to impede its full power. The temperature soared to 101 degrees.

Nobody was happy. Rather than enjoy a lengthy time of relaxation together, we were forced to leave earlier than we wanted. I drove my wife and kids to my childhood home. Though they were crabby and worn out, this was their only opportunity to see it. I sensed there was a very real possibility that there would be no future occasion for them to catch a glimpse of my childhood. Rather than the experience being a time of discovery, however, they were exasperated by the stifling and all-consuming heat.

I carefully walked them over a bottomless sea of countless belongings, carrying them individually in places, so they could peek their heads into my former bedroom. The room was piled so high with debris that it was impossible to fully open the door or step inside. Standing atop junk in the hallway that had shrunk to the width of a single person, I held each of my twins up one at a time so they could peek inside. My son and daughter were aghast, and were not interested in lingering. Before panic could set in, I evacuated my wife and children from the claustrophobic house. They waited outside as they melted down emotionally from heat and stress.

Inside, Enoch was busily showing me all his projects that had improved the place. I was unable to break away as my wife barely held things together outside where the temperature remained above 100 degrees. In the worst timing imaginable, which is when these things always seem to happen, my daughter slammed her fingers in the car door. Shawna was reduced to the impossible position I had been in years earlier as she lay passed out in my arms on the floor of a public restroom of the gas station a few miles away from what should have been relief. She was forced to explain to our seven-year-old daughter why they weren't able to go back into Grandma's house to obtain ice to soothe her sore hand. The time dragged on as the tour continued inside. Both kids wanted nothing more than to return to our campground so they could swim at the nearby lake.

One of my cousins—whom I hadn't seen in 13 years, and only briefly at my wedding—was getting married. Relations with my extended family were virtually non-existent due to complications described herein and that could fill another book. I decided it was time to venture down to take part in the nuptials while also visiting my mom. Though the wedding was near Milwaukee, only a short drive from Grandma's house, we were forced to camp instead. The experience gave the expression "Hot as Hell" new meaning. It was like living in Purgatory for the entire three-day stay. There were zero opportunities to get inside out of the heat to relax. The atmosphere inside our tent was stifling all night long. The temperatures outside stubbornly remained at or near 90 degrees even after dark, and our body heat kept the inside of our cramped four-man tent above 100. We all laid nearly nude on top of a sheet, doing our best not to allow any part of our nasty, sweaty bodies to touch. This was Hell on earth, and something I don't plan on enduring again.

It was worth it, though. I was grateful to connect with my extended family for the first time since permanently leaving home so many years earlier. Feeling a bit like a black sheep, I was deeply honored to be chosen as a pallbearer when grandfather died a year later. I had done nothing to deserve such an honor. I made the trip alone, and was touched more than the family can possibly realize.

I have only scratched the surface in describing how difficult it is to arrange visits with my kids' grandma. They deserve to have a relationship with her, and she with them. Not having a home base to return to while visiting produces profound inconvenience and frustration. The main issue is that finding a relaxing place to get out of the wind, cold, or heat always involves shelling out cash at restaurants or hotels. It's miserable. A trip to visit my dad feels impossible for another reason; his shedding dog triggers allergies in the family. Decades of dust in the home once occupied by my grandma and grandpa has accumulated in all the bedding, curtains, and furniture as well. Thus, I carry guilt for rarely arranging visits to the homes of either grandparent. After all, my own stays with Grandma and Grandpa were one of the few sources of joy and stability in my life as a child. Thankfully we have opportunities to enjoy more normal visits with my wife's family, but I try not to speak of these much, out of fear my parents will become jealous.

I listen with rapt attention when other people talk about taking their children to visit grandparents. I draw out every detail I can from them, and get the sense that they must think I'm being overly interested in such mundane matters. On the contrary, I find them to be exotically fascinating. It grieves me that we can't even consider traveling to visit my mom for a weekend. I am unaware of anyone else on earth that faces such a predicament, but I'm certain they exist. If that is you, take heart dear brother or sister. I relate to you entirely, and send a warm hug. You can still be a fantastic parent. Be vulnerable with your kids. Let them see the full scope of your humanity, warts and all. They will appreciate you all the more because of it.

Frequently I am sobered by the realization that apples aren't usually catapulted from the proverbial tree. I certainly have plenty of "issues" to deal with myself. I love both my parents even though they frustrate me endlessly. Dad says I got the "angry gene" from my mom. Unfortunately, nearly all his photos of me—glaring or scowling at the camera in exasperation—bear this out to some degree. Though I seem to spend the lion's share of our scant time together lecturing or yelling at them, I cannot imagine having any other parents. They are the ones I have been given, and dare I say it, am blessed with. Though they have deficiencies, I have always known they love me. Despite their crazy eccentricities, I love them dearly. I long for them to experience lives marked by joy, discovery, and fulfillment. Of course I am not able to mold them into my own conception of what such a life looks like. I simply need to love them for who they are.

Due to my adventurous escape from a life of poverty, lack of meaning, and confusion, I will not take for granted this wonderful life I've been blessed with. My family and I cherish each other. We live in a 105-year-old home with character, and I'm not ashamed to invite people in to share our lives. The endless sorting of trinkets and possessions is not the defining work of my life. I am free to explore hobbies and interests to my heart's content. These are beautiful things that have eluded my mother. In the interest of sparing her some dignity, I'll leave the critique there.

ACKNOWLEDGEMENTS

I have dreamed of writing this book for 19 years. Following the crisis of my job loss, several individuals went above and beyond the normal call of duty in helping to make this dream a reality.

John Baker. Dude, thank you so much. Sure, I would have published this thing a couple years ago without you, but it would have been an anticlimactic dud. Thank you so much for pushing me to make this book into much more than it was. Your suggestions and very fine editing work have been invaluable. If you had slept in the middle of the same animal menagerie, as the brother that I never had, I'd say this book was as much yours as it is mine. You've come pretty close to that. The fact that you've spent hundreds of hours assisting me on this FOR FREE is remarkable. You are a great friend, and I'm certain our friendship will last a lifetime. Any mistakes within this humble piece of work are my own.

Mom, I love you. Thanks for being courageous and supportive of my work on this story. You recognize this is just my story. I know you have generally done your best in life. Now perhaps you can move on to something more though! It's now or never. Of course, you realize this. I appreciate you continuing to at least listen politely to my pleas for change! Dare to dream big. You have nothing to lose.

I love you too Dad. You are one crazy son of a gun, and though you drive me nuts, your differentness is what sets you apart. Thank you for being you. Your chapter is as long as it is for a reason. Your impact on my life has been incalculable.

Enoch, please know that what I've written isn't personal. It's just the telling of my story as it happened, and from the viewpoint of a child. I realize that you have positive qualities as well as the mostly negative ones described herein. For example, I remain grateful that you have been there for my mom throughout various crises when she literally had nobody else to turn to. I do not know what would have become of her if you hadn't been in her life during those crucial junctures. You have been very helpful to her in practical ways. However, the key to winning my mother's heart is pretty simple: tender, loving-kindness. It's still possible. Portions of this book may be unpalatable to both you and Mom. Good medicine often doesn't taste yummy. I hope my words and memories provoke meaningful reflection and positive change for you both.

A hearty thanks is sent to Naomi Christenson for her fine design work with the cover and interior. I certainly would have freaked out during the publishing process if it weren't for your guiding hand. To Aaron Peterson, Ryan Underwood, and Anna Bailey, I also extend gratitude for making the audiobook version possible. Seriously.
Thank you.

Finally, I wish to thank the following individuals for their undying encouragement. You all have been invaluable in helping me finally bring this bastard to completion. So without further ado, and with apologies to numerous folks that I must be forgetting (I'm only human mind you) Dan, Ryan, Keith, and Melanie, thank you from the bottom of my heart. I also wish to add all my neighbors to this list. Thank you for your unwavering encouragement, and also for being a vital part of my story.

And finally, Shawna. Thank you for being the love of my life, for supporting this project from beginning to end, and for your lovely painting on the cover. I am grateful that you and the kids are central elements within the ongoing story. Life is such an adventure with you all.

ABOUT THE AUTHOR

With 19 years of bedwetting experience under his belt, and a childhood spent enduring a broken home so cluttered with rotting detritus that piles nearly reached the ceiling, Eddy Gilmore has been gifted with a unique perspective on life. He lives in Duluth, Minnesota, where he writes a newspaper column and loves to play along the shores of Lake Superior with his wife and children.

Discover more at eddygilmore.com.